Edward R. Taylor

Something of Value for Every Farmer

gardener, ranchman, florist and flour miller

Edward R. Taylor

Something of Value for Every Farmer
gardener, ranchman, florist and flour miller

ISBN/EAN: 9783337315924

Printed in Europe, USA, Canada, Australia, Japan

Cover: Foto ©Lupo / pixelio.de

More available books at **www.hansebooks.com**

Taylor's "Fuma" Carbon Bisulfide

Kills Weevil in . . .

WHEAT, CORN, PEAS, BEANS, RICE, Etc.

Insects in Furs, Clothes, Furniture, Etc.

"Why stand idly by while myriads of insects eat what has cost so much labor to harvest"? Weed

The best remedy in every respect for killing grain insects is Bisulfide of Carbon. It is cheap, effective, and easy to apply. — Bulletin 79 Arizona Exp. Station.

YOU CAN EXTERMINATE

Woodchucks, Prairie Dogs, Gophers, Squirrels, and Rats without leaving one to tell the tale.

Ind rsed by the U. S. Dept of Agriculture and by the State Experiment Stations

This Pamphlet sent free on application to

EDWARD R. TAYLOR, Penn Yan, N. Y.

Directions for Using Fuma to Kill Insects in Mills.

Use not less than 100 lbs. for a two story 30x40 foot structure. Double the amount if badly infested. Increase the amount in the same proportion for larger structures. Open buildings require much more than tight ones.

Clean the mill, have as little flour, feed, etc., in mill, conveyors, machines, etc., as possible. Open the doors of bolts, place a small shelf up in the flour packer, flour **bins**, etc.; borrow fifty soup plates from your merchant for **each 50 pounds to be** used (can be returned **unharmed**); (do not use **deep dishe.—the evaporation is too slow**), go through the mill and select places to put them. Place them high up when practicable, as the vapor is 2½ times heavier than air and descends, and the vapor, not the liquid, does the work, but it must be thick enough for the evaporation from the numerous plates to produce a **death atmosphere**. Commence at the bottom **floor and work up**. Place plates above the bolts, etc. One person can fill and two place them. Take bunches of **cotton waste of** about ¼ pound weight, saturate and place in top of conveyors, machines, etc. Be expeditious about the work, keep the liquid down and heads up, to avoid breathing the vapor unnecessarily. You need not be **afraid** of it simply avoid breathing it. Set a saucer or shallow vessel, with a little in, near cracks and infested corners. See that all windows and doors are shut. For a grain bin say 10x10x10, pour two pounds in four places near the **four** corners. Do the work Saturday afternoon by **daylight**. **Absolutely** have no **Lights or Fire of any** kind about. Close the **mill and leave** the bugs to **their** destruction until Monday morning. Then open doors **and windows** and thoroughly ventilate before going to work.

I would emphasize the **use of** saturated cotton waste wherever practicable, as a very effective method of application.

Spraying with sprinkling pots **in corners**, cracks and infested places is a most effective way, but you must be expeditious.

For **grain** pour directly into the mass in several places, allowing **about** 1½ gallons—15 pounds—to each one thousand bushels. Cover closely to confine the fumes.

(When **not in** use keep drums tightly sealed. Use hard soap on plug **to seal** it.)

Louisville, Neb., Dec. 5, **1898**.

Edward R. Taylor, Cleveland, O.

Enclosed find draft for $5. **Your Fuma is all right;** it does the work. I shall recommend it to our farmers; that is the place we get the weevil from. The next time I shall **order 10 gallons**. I think it will fix mice and everything else.

LOUISVILLE MILLING CO.

TO DESTROY INSECTS IN STORED GRAIN.

(PROF. HOWARD EVARTS WEED, Mississippi Experiment Station.)

Although corn and other grain is at times severely injured in the field by many insects, it is attacked by even more injurious species when in the granary. The application of various remedies will greatly lessen the damage done by insects to grain in the field. These remedies consist of the application of insecticides, rotation of crops, clean culture, and the planting of trap crops. For the insects in the granary, however, there is but one remedy, and this remedy is so good, simple and perfect, that no other is needed or indeed wanted. This remedy consists in the application of Bisulfide of Carbon to the stored grain. Properly speaking, it is a preventive to insect injury rather than a remedy, since it prevents further damage to the grain by killing the insects which infest it.

But before describing details as to the application of the Bisulfide of Carbon, perhaps it will be best to first consider the manner in which insects infesting grain do their work. Although there are many species of insects which infest stored grain, yet their life-history and manner of work are essentially the same, so that we may take only one as an example of all. Thus we may consider the black weevil, which probably is the species doing the most damage to corn throughout the Southern States, while a near related species does the greatest damage in the Northern States. The life-history of the black weevil is as follows:

The eggs are laid by the female weevils at the soft part of the kernels near the cob, and in a few days these eggs hatch into small wrinkled larvæ which feed within the kernels. At a in the accompanying figure is shown the larva much enlarged. The larvæ feed for about four weeks when they are ready to form pupæ, which they do within the kernels. A pupa is shown at b in the illustration, and as may be seen from this figure it presents nearly the same outline as the mature weevil, excepting that the wings are folded around and under the body. In about ten days the pupæ change into the weevils, one of them being shown much enlarged at c. The weevil is so familiar that no description is necessary here, the principal point being the

REMEDY FOR STORED GRAIN INSECTS.

This, as already stated, consists in the application of Bisulfide of Carbon. This substance is a liquid and of a volatile nature. It kills by means of its deadly fumes, and on this account is an excellent insecticide for use against insects confined within something where the insects cannot be reached by the ordinary insecticides, such as Paris green and the like. The fumes of the Bisulfide are heavier than air, and the best mode of application is simply to pour it over the top of the grain. Some place it in an open vessel at the bottom of the crib or grain bin before the grain is put in, thus allowing the Bisulfide to evaporate slowly. But this latter method, however, is not as easily done as is the application of the Bisulfide by simply pouring it over the top of the grain. When this is done, the fumes penetrate all parts of the grain and will evaporate in the course of a few hours, leaving destruction in its path.

The Bisulfide is inflammable, and lights, lighted cigars, and the like, should not be brought near until the odor of the Bisulfide has passed off, which will be within twenty-four hours. When grain is treated in this way, the germinating power of the seed is not injured and no damage is done to the grain in any way.

Bisulfide of Carbon can be obtained at the drug stores at a cost of from 25 to 60 cents per pound, depending on how large a profit each druggist may make. It can be obtained direct from the manufacturer, Edward R. Taylor in fifty-pound cans, at 10 cents per pound. As the Bisulfide is also useful to destroy ants and many other insects, it should be kept on hand upon a farm for use as occasion may require. The amount to be used when treating grain in any given case will depend upon circumstances, the amount of grain, its nature, and the tightness of the bin or crib containing it. Pour on what you think is enough, and then examine two days later, and if all the weevils are not killed, make another application, this time using more. Of course, when the grain is in a tight bin, it will take less Bisulfide for the treatment than when the grain is in an open crib. Heretofore it has been recommended that about an ounce of Bisulfide to the hundred pounds of grain, or a pound to the ton, should be used, but late experience has shown that this amount is not necessary, as a much smaller amount will do the work.

This remedy for grain insects is very simple and costs but little. Then why stand idly by while myriads of insects eat the grain that has taken so much labor to harvest? The weevils are generally within the grain when harvested, or they may also get into it afterward. In the early summer when the supply of grain is nearly exhausted in the cribs or granaries there are always many insects ready to escape to begin their work upon the grain in the field; or, in case the supply of grain is not exhausted in the granaries before the new crop is gathered, the insects will remain in the granaries throughout the season. Thus the granaries should be cleaned out well before a new crop is gathered. This should be done as soon as the grain is nearly exhausted, and any weevils which may be upon the bottom of the granary should be carefully swept up and killed by placing in a pail containing kerosene. This is very important, as it will very greatly lessen the number of the insects a little later.—*Industrial American.*

FIRST LARVAL STAGE OF THE PEA WEEVIL.

[*Insect Life, Vol. V, No. 5, page 295.*]

Bruchus pisi L., first larval stage; *a*, egg on pod; *b*, cross-section of opening of mine; *c*, young larva and opening on inside of pod by which it has entered—enlarged; *d, d, d*, eggs—natural size, *e*, first larva—greatly enlarged; *f*, postembryonic leg; *g*, prothoracic spinous process s—still more enlarged (original.)

The fact that the Pea Weevil deposits its egg on the outside of the pod, fastening it thereto, has long been known, and we have found, as we surmised would be the case, that the newly-hatched larva of this species has the same characteristics as those we have described in the case of the Bean Weevil.

An interesting fact connected with this larva is, that while ordinarily entering the pea direct from the amber-colored egg, as previously recorded, it sometimes enters the pod in the neighborhood of the egg and then mines along the inside of the pod for some distance, being quite active and moving rapidly and with ease. This doubtless occurs whenever the egg hatches before the peas are sufficiently developed, the larva living as a miner until the pea is nearly full grown, and the entrance of the larva into a pea in such case would seem to be rather by chance than by design. As in the case of the Bean Weevil, however, the larva molts and loses its legs and other post-embryonic characters as soon as it has entered the pea.—*From Insect Life, Vol. 4, page 392.*

THE PEA WEEVIL.

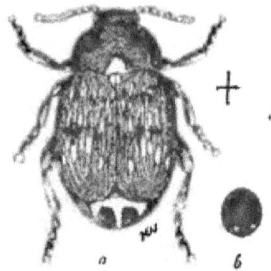

In the article we show the pea weevil also the bean weevil (*Bruchus Pisarum*) greatly enlarged, also a pea, showing the puncture of the legume. The pea weevil is widely disseminated over the United States. The same means of extermination will be applicable as given above for the bean weevil.

WEEVILS IN PEAS.

When peas or beans are stored over winter to be planted the following season, they become infested with weevils of a similiar nature to the ones which are found in corn and other grain. While the weevils in peas and beans are of different species scientifically from the weevils in corn, yet to all intents and purposes, they are the same so far as their destructive influences are concerned. The common bean weevil is shown much enlarged at c in figure 1, d showing a bean in which the weevil has been at work. The species which works in our cow peas is very similar to this, and as a rule the peas are infested with weevils when they are gathered from the field. The weevils continue their growth and propagate in the peas when stored, and in many cases by the time spring opens, the peas will be destroyed.

REMEDY FOR THESE INSECTS.

There is no occasion for any loss by these insects, for the simple remedy given last month for the corn weevils, is also applicable to these pea weevils. So the remedy is simply this: Pour a small amount of Bisulfide of Carbon over the infested peas. This is best done by placing the peas in a box or a grain bin, so that the fumes of the Bisulfide will be confined as much as possible. But a small amount of the Bisulfide will be needed in the treatment of a large bin of the peas, so that the cost of treatment is very little.—*From Southern Cultivator, page 533, Nov. 1894.*

THE BEAN WEEVIL AND BISULFIDE OF CARBON.

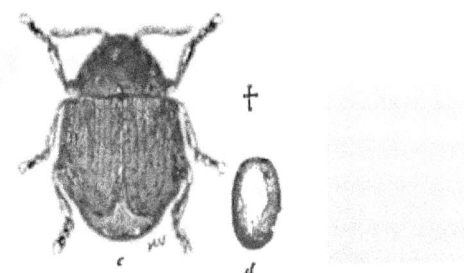

[*From The Prairie Farmer of Oct. 1, 1892.*]

Of this comparatively recent insect, as known in the United States—1860—but which has caused much trouble because infesting the seeds of the bean plant, and even breeding therein, and from the fact that the means of destroying them is before the beans are stored away, we find a most comprehensive and elaborate history and description of this pest in the seventh annual report of injurious insects of New York, by J. A. Lintner, Ph. D., State Entomologist.

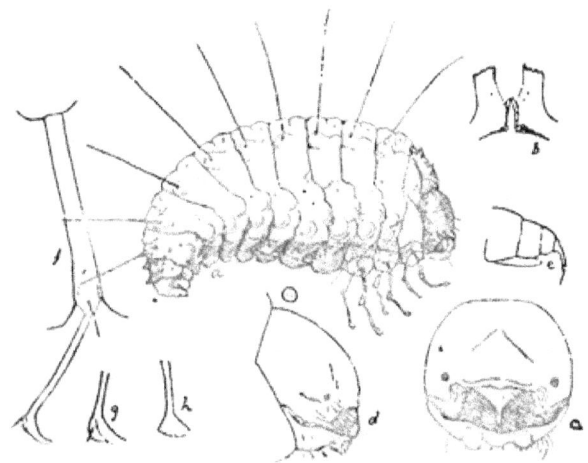

LARVAL STAGE OF BEAN WEEVIL.

Said description of the beetle is as follows:

Body blackish cinereous with a slight tinge of brown; antennæ ot deeply serrate; thorax much narrowed before, cinereous each side, a slight impressed dorsal line; base with the edge almost angulated, central lobe almost truncate; scutel quadrate, whitish, longitudinally divided by a dusky line; elytra with the intersticial lines having a slight appearance of alternating whitish and dusky; on the middle of the third intersticial line is a more abbreviated whitish line; posterior thighs with a black spine and two smaller ones.

Length over one-tenth of an inch.

The whitish or cinereous markings are not very striking; on the elytra they may sometimes be traced into two obselete macular bands.

The above, and reference to the cut, will be sufficient means for identifying the insect. It is needless to say that infested beans or peas are unfit for food, and that sowing infested seed will multiply the evil. Hence, coming now to the means of destruction. Of the various means there is only one safe and easily used agent where the beans are to be used as a food. This is Bisulfide of Carbon. It is also the best medium for the destruction of insect life in all insect-infested seeds or grains.

Exposure to the vapor of this volatile liquid is an infallible means of killing our bean and pea weevils. The infested beans may be put in some tight vessel, box, or bin, with a cup containing Bisulfide of Carbon upon them, covering up closely and leaving them for a day or two. The heavy vapor—about two and one-half times heavier than common air—given off will descend and kill all the animal life present, without injury to the germ, or impairment for use as food after suitable exposure to the air. This valuable insecticide—available against a large number of our insect enemies —may be purchased at drug stores at the moderate price, by the pound, of about thirty cents. A small quantity of it will suffice. It has been found, in experiments on a large scale made in India for killing the weevils that there infest stored grain quite seriously, that one pound and a half is amply sufficient for use in a ton of grain, provided that the grain is inclosed in tight vessels. As the vapor is quite inflammable, precaution should always be taken not to bring a light in contact with it.

The sooner the remedy can be applied to the infested beans after their ripening and gathering, the greater will be their value for food. As at that early time, the presence of the insect within is not so readily detected, it would be wise, if in all localities where it has obtained a foothold, that examination be made before storing, either by careful inspection of the surface, or, what would be preferable, opening a number and examining their interior.

It is evident in the light that we now have, that this pest may not be exterminated from a locality by the refraining, by common consent, for a year or two, from the culture of the bean, as we have previously recommended, for the insect may be safely "tided over" during that time by continued generation within the stored crops, or in the housewife's bag of beans carefully laid aside and protected in some bye and forgotton drawer.

The Tracy House. - Perhaps in no way could as much be accomplished toward arresting the spread of this insect, as in the use, by all extensive bean-growers, of the "Tracy house," or "bug-house," which, according to Professor A. J. Cook, was largely used by the pea-growers of Northern New York for the arrest of the ravages of the pea weevil, when not long ago the pea interest was threatened with destruction. Professor Cook has given the following description of the house and the manner in which the Bisulfide of Carbon is used in it, in *Bulletin* No. 58, Michigan Agricultural Experiment Station:

."The house is made air-tight; even the door is made very close-fitting; and is made still closer by pasting paper over the edges upon closing it, after filling the house with sacks of peas. An air-tight flue at one end opens at the very top into the building, and at the bottom out of doors. A sort of chute with an adjustable air-tight valve is arranged for the turning in of the liquid. The liquid is turned in till the odor shows that the vapor is pouring out at the bottom of the flue. Then, of course, the air has been all forced out by the vapor when the valve is closed. It is left closed for three days; then the doors are opened that the vapor may escape, when all the weevils will be dead."

Prof. M. V. Slingerland in *Insect Life*, vol. 5, page 87, regarding Bean Weevil, says:

Bisulfide of Carbon destroys all stages, Insect Eggs, Larvæ of all sizes, Pupæ and all adults.

CHICKEN LICE.

Editor Dixie Miller:

If you would please make known my experience with the chicken lice in your valuable paper, it would help some of your readers. I live on high, sandy land, and have had always 20 to 50 chickens. Last fall and winter lice became so numerous that we tried in succession kerosene, quick lime, hot water, insect powder, tar, salt in every form, etc, with no visible benefit. I read several articles on Bisulfide of Carbon, but no drug store would keep the cheap kind for this purpose.

Meanwhile, I concluded to send on to the manufacturer, E. R. Taylor who sent me some, and I tried it in small bottles, which were left to evaporate; and after a week I refilled, and so again the third week, when I could see that all the flees disappeared by degrees.

We were delighted, as we could not go to the chicken house, the road was so covered with the pests. To put the foot one second in the sand was enough to cover them with little fleas. I hope no one else will have so many, but there are a great many in this State who cannot keep poultry to advantage for this pest.

Hoping you will use this whenever convenient, as I am ready to vouch for it at any time, I remain

Respectfully yours,

Winterhaven, Fla.   CARL NIEDERER.

CARBON BISULFIDE FOR HEN LICE.

The following is from Dr. Schneider, in the Paris *Journal de l'Agriculture* on Sulfide of Carbon for destroying lice :

"The very next day after using it I was agreeably surprised to find that the enemy had left leaving none but dead and dying behind, and on the following day not a single living insect was to be found, while my birds were sitting quietly on the roosts enjoying an unwontedly peaceful repose. This lasted for twelve days, till the Sulfide had evaporated. Twenty four hours later a fresh invasion of lice had put in an appearance under the wings of the birds in the warmest portions of the house, where there were no currents of air. I replenished the supply of Sulfide, and the next morning only a few of these were remaining. The next morning every trace of the vermin had disappeared. Since that time I have personally made a great number of further trials with the Sulfide, with immediate and absolute success. I should recommend the Sulfide of Carbon to be put in small medicine vials hung about the pigeon house or poultry roost. When it has about three parts evaporated the remainder will have acquired a yellowish tinge, and no longer acts so completely as before, but if it be shaken up afresh it will suffice to keep the enemy at a distance."

In relation to the above Mr. Taylor says:

"I should think a few small bottles of it tied to the perches as indicated, would be very efficient, as when the chickens roost their feathers would come almost down to the mouth of the bottle; though the vapor naturally goes down, the law of diffusion of gases will cause enough of it to go upward to be sufficient, as the writer indicates."

I have used Bisulfide of Carbon for the common gray and small red lice, and never found anything to equal it for effectiveness and ease of application. Place in open mouth vials and hang them under the roost, using one vial for from four to six feet of roost, and you will find no lice in twenty-four hours; at least this is my experience. It evaporates soon, and should be replaced in a couple of weeks. W. H. BIDDLE, in *The Epitomist*.

Mr. Cash, Asst. Director Experimental Farm No. 2, Idaho Falls, writes as follows:

"The 'Carbon' was used with marked success in disposing of chicken lice and bed bugs where everything else had failed. Sprinkled on the walls and floor, and the room closed up tightly for a short time, the vermin all leave, never to return."

BISULFIDE OF CARBON.—Mr. J. F. Deyoe, of Oregon, writes THE FARMERS VOICE: "The Bisulfide of Carbon which you recommend for chicken lice is the best and cheapest and the least trouble to use of anything I ever tried. I can't say too much in praise of it. It freed my hennery from lice in 24 hours. I think it will do up the red mites just as quick."

OCCURRENCE OF THE HEN FLEA (Sarcopsylla Gallinacea Westw.) IN FLORIDA.

[*From Insect Life.*]

By A. S. PACKARD, Providence, R. I.

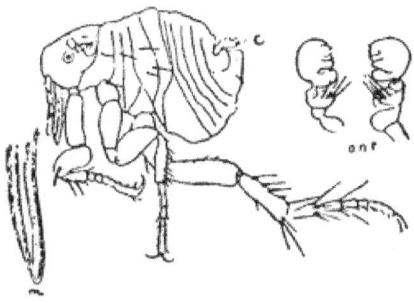

Fig. 8. *Sarcopsylla gallinacea*. Male—enlarged; *ant*, antennæ; *m*, palpi—more enlarged. (From drawings by Packard.)

DEATH TO CHICKEN LICE.

I use bisulphide of carbon in preference to anything else for killing chicken lice. I have used it four years, and I think it the best thing yet discovered for that purpose. Before I used it, my chicken house was literally alive with mites, but in 24 hours after I applied the carbon, I could not find one. I fill several three or four-ounce vials one-half full of the carbon, have them uncorked, and tie a string to the neck of each long enough to let it hang from 12 to 20 inches below the perches. I have enough vials to hang about six to eight feet apart, and refill the vials about every week or as often as the stuff evaporates.

Canby, Oregon. J. F. D.

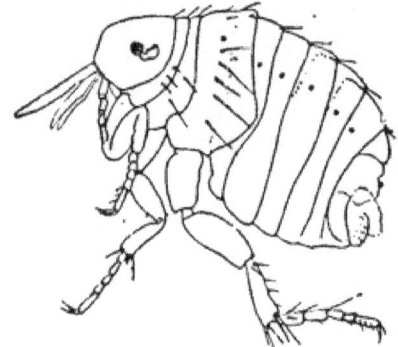

Fig. 9. *Sarcopsylla gallinacea*: Female—enlarged.
(From drawings by Packard.)

REMEDY FOR TEXAS FLEAS.

[*Southern Cultivator*, Page 506, October, 1894.]

Please advise me what will rid mules, chickens, etc., of Texas fleas.—A. C. F., Jr., Montezuma, Ga.

ANSWER.--Mr. Carl Niederer, of Winter Haven, Fla., gives us his experience with fleas, which may prove of advantage to our inquirer. Mr. Niederer writes that all last winter he was bothered with chicken fleas. In vain he tried insect powder, gas lime, boiling water, kerosene, potash, salt and carbolic acid mixed with lard. The fleas multiplied until they reached the dwelling house, 12 feet away from the chicken house. Reading in the bulletin of an agricultural experiment station; a recommendation of Bisulfide of Carbon, and noting the advertisement of Mr. E. R. Taylor, of Cleveland, Ohio, in *The Cultivator*, he sent on for twenty pounds of Taylor's Carbon Bisulfide. He put in about an ounce of the Bisulfide in each of eight bottles, and leaving them uncorked, hung them on the roost. There was no perceptible effect the first week. The second week Mr. Niederer filled the bottles about one-third full, and let it evaporate. At the end of the week the effect was beginning to show, and at the end of the third week the fleas were all gone. While all other remedies failed, the Bisulfide was a complete success.

FUR ANIMALS.

Fur animals such as Mink, Foxes, Coyotes, Badger, Skunk, Muskrats, etc., whose fur is of value, they can be dug out 24 hours after treatment and the skins obtained intact, and in case of skunks without smell, which to most people would be quite an object.

POCKET-GOPHERS.

From Farm and Fireside.

W. D. P., Wellfleet, Neb., writes: "Kindly inform me what animal eats off the roots of orchard trees—roots as thick as a man's wrist. What are the habits of said animal, and what is the way to guard against ravages? I think it is the pocket-gopher, but am not sure."

REPLY:—Your trees were undoubtedly destroyed by the pocket-gopher. I have seen many trees destroyed in the same way in neglected orchards. This animal lives entirely underground, where it burrows in a manner similar to the mole of the eastern states, only since it is often five times as large as a mole its burrows are the more harmful. As it burrows it throws up piles of soil every four or five feet, so that its presence is easily known. It feeds on vegetable matter almost exclusively, and so far as I know has not a single redeeming feature, while the mole and shrew are beneficial in that they feed largely on grubs and other animals. My practice is to watch for their marks on the outskirts of the orchard, and as soon as seen, to open the burrow and put in a piece of cotton batting saturated with about a tablespoonful of Bisulfide of Carbon, and then cover the hole with an inverted sod. The vapor of this material is very heavy and sure death to animal life. It costs about one dollar a gallon, and is about as dangerous to use around a fire as gasoline. It is the most satisfactory thing I have tried for this pest. Another way that I used to practice besides trapping, is to cut an apple, carrot or potato, cover the cut surface with strychnine and put it on a pointed stick and lay in the burrow.

Editor American Elevator and Grain Trade:—I noticed the article in the *American Elevator and Grain Trade* about the Texas man and his box with a bottle of Bisulfide of Carbon in his grain bins. It is a remarkable fact that the great success with Bisulfide of Carbon in killing rats in Paris, France, was what led to its extensive use in the West for killing prairie dogs. I am positive its great value for killing rats is not at all appreciated in this country. In its use, however, for killing rats, it must be remembered that they are made to live in close places and the foulest air in which any animal can live, and anyone who tries to dispose of them with it *must persist.*

Three years ago my barn was overrun with them. The first treatment seemed a failure, for, though appearing somewhat dazed they seemed as plenty as ever. If it would not kill them, I, of all men, wanted to know it, and I gave them three more doses within ten days, and they gave up and I have not seen a rat about the place since. The place must have a bad reputation in the rat kingdom. The best way to treat them is to saturate cotton waste with Bisulfide of Carbon, push it into their earthholes and cover the holes. If they dig the cotton out give them some more. Where they cannot be got at under buildings only a foot or two above the ground, a modification of the Texas man's plan might serve to kill them, as the vapor is heavy and in such a place would ultimately travel to the bottom of their holes. There would be no danger of fire in such use, if there were no openings the vapor would travel through to fire at the same or at a lower level. E. R. TAYLOR.

THE FUMA, OR BISULPHIDE OF CARBON.

The advertisement of this, which appears in our present issue, is surely the greatest thing in the way of an insecticide that has yet been discovered. We have repeatedly mentioned its wonderful property of killing the weevil in beans and peas, even before they have eaten through the seed. Recent investigations by our experiment stations and others have shown that it is the cheapest and most effective remedy for almost every insect or animal pest that afflicts the farmer or horticulturist. We used to pay 40 or 50 cents a pound for the drug; but it is now offered in quantities for less than one-fourth that price. There should be no excuse now for having insects, rats, or mice in our houses, barns, cellars, granaries, or anywhere else. It is not often that we give so much space toward helping an advertiser; but this is a recent product of unusual merit.— A. I. Root, Cor., Bee Journal.

TO DESTROY GOPHERS, GROUND-HOGS, ETC.

For exterminating burrowing animals, such as gophers, groundhogs, moles, etc., we know of nothing equal to bisulfide of carbon. Saturate a handful of rags or a ball of cotton with this liquid, roll it into the burrow and close up the opening tightly with earth. For moles, dig open their runs, put in a saturated ball each way and close up with earth. The heavy vapor of this volatile liquid is sure death to insects and animals. Send to E. R. Taylor, Penn Yan, N. Y., for pamphlet on Bisulfide of Carbon.
S. A. SILVERDALE,
Ontario, Can.

THE EXTERMINATION OF GOPHERS.

CARBON BISULPHIDE AS AN EXTERMINATOR.

[Report of the Chemist, Canada Department of Agriculture, Central Experimental Farm.]

"A method that is strongly advocated by those who have practiced it in the United States is one employing carbon bisulfide. It is held to be cheaper, more efficacious and less dangerous to use than strychnine.

"Carbon bisulfide is a highly inflammable liquid, with a very disagreeable smell. Though not corrosive, its vapor is detrimental to health when breathed in quantities. It however, can be used without any danger, provided ordinary care is exercised—more especially with regard to fire and flame.

"The method is as follows: Saturate a small ball of cotton waste with the bisulfide, and throw it into the burrow in the evening; then close the mouth of the hole with earth.

"Dry balls of horse manure have been used successfully instead of cotton."

Respecting this method, I would make two quotations. Dr. C. Hart Merriam, Chief of the Division of Ornithology and Mammalogy, Washington, D. C., writes me as follows:—

"As a general rule, we do not recommend either arsenic or strychnine for the extermination of pocket gophers. We prefer the sulfide of carbon as cheaper and more efficacious. A handful of rags or wet waste wet with the bisulfide should be thrust into a fresh burrow; the mouth of the burrow should then be stopped. The fumes from the bisulfide being heavier than the atmospheric air, float down along the tunnel to its utmost ramifications, destroying all animals there."

"In a letter from Prof. Niswander, of the Wyoming Experiment Station, I have the following testimony:—

"Over 2,000 burrows have been treated by me in 1893 by bisulfide, and 99 per cent. of the trials have been successful.

"In a few instances the holes have been apparently opened from the outside, and these were all counted with the unsatisfactory trials. I have no hesitation in recommending carbon bisulfide for burrowing animals."

Further, he says:

"The most important thing in the use of strychnine is to get the gophers to eat it; with the bisulfide this is not necessary. Both arsenic and strychnine are dangerous to stock running loose, the bisulfide entails no such risk."

After the hay is up and the oats taken care of, a couple of days can be spent to excellent advantage in killing off the gophers that disfigure the meadows with their hills. About the easiest way to fight them is by the use of chemicals and the most effective of these is carbon bisulphide, as recommended by state and governmental entomologists. Concerning it Dr. Merriam, of the division of Ornithology, Washington, D. C., writes: "As a general rule, we do not recommend either arsenic or strychnine for the extermination of pocket gophers. We prefer the sulfide of carbon as cheaper and more efficacious. A handful of rags or waste wet with the bisulfide should be thrust into a fresh burrow; the mouth of the burrow should then be stopped. The fumes from the bisulfide being heavier than atmospheric air, float down along the tunnel to its remotest ramifications, destroying all animals there."

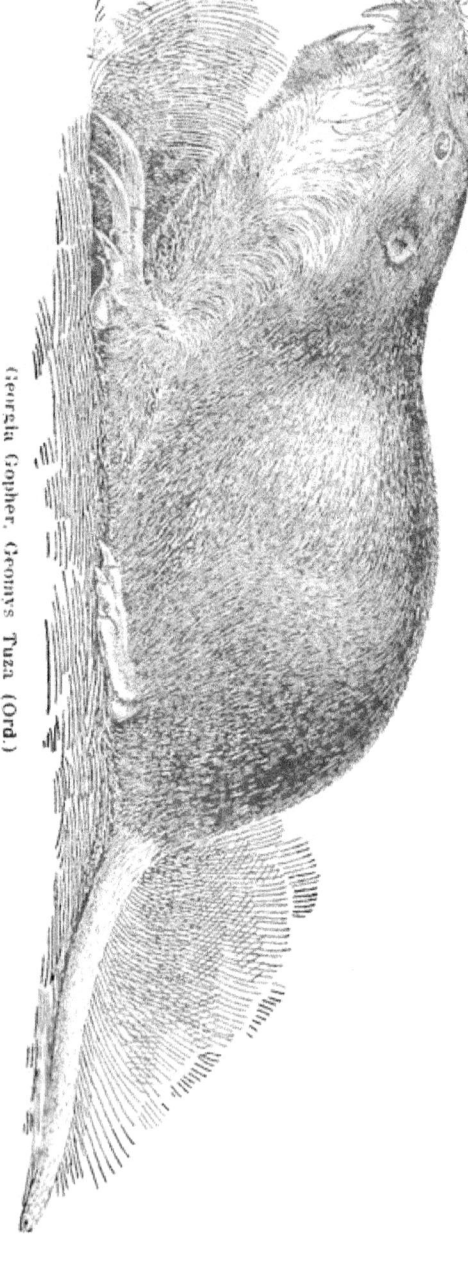

Farm Bulletin No. 5, Division of Ornithology and Mammalogy, Department of Agriculture.

Georgia Gopher, Geomys Tuza (Ord.)

BISULFIDE OF CARBON FOR BURROWING ANIMALS.

Mr. R. E. Beatty, Arapahoe County, Col., writes: I wish to make it known through the *Prairie Farmer* the complete success of Bisulfide of Carbon to exterminate ground squirrels, gophers, etc. Take a cotton ball, saturate it with the liquid, roll into the hole, close up tight, and it is a sure shot every time. For moles dig down to their runs and put in a saturated ball both ways, close the hole, and it will kill them. But moles are hard to get rid of, and you must be attentive and do the work thoroughly, as you cannot find all the holes at once, but by watching you can see their mounds as they dig up the dirt. Ground squirrels can be completely exterminated by applying it in their burrows, and every one knows the destruction they make with newly-planted corn in Colorado. We are troubled with prairie dogs, and they are very destructive on crops of all kinds—in fact, they would completely ruin grain or corn if it were not for some remedy to rid the field of them. The best remedy is Fuma, which is a preparation of Bisulfide. Use Fuma. It is better for killing all rodents. I hope some of your readers will be induced to try it, and report through your paper, as it is the best remedy in existence. I had 160 acres completely overrun with prairie dogs. They ruined the pasture and almost destroyed my corn crop. I procured 150 pounds of Fuma Bisulfide and completely rid the field of them. All use it around this section of the country, and with complete success. It is used also to kill weevil in grain. It is not costly, and should be used by everyone that is troubled with rodents of any kind. It will kill skunks, rabbits or weasels. To those wishing to use it, I would recommend them to Edward R. Taylor, as he is the manufacturer, and he will send you pamphlets describing the various uses that it can be applied to.

GOOD-BY TO WOODCHUCKS.

Reading in a government report that a number of townships in the west had been cleared of gophers by the use of Bisulfide of Carbon, I tried it for woodchucks with gratifying results. Buy a can of Bisulfide of Carbon, pour three or four tablespoonfuls into a bottle and cork it up tight. Visit the hole when the family are in. Close one opening and insert a handful of rags in the other as far as can be reached. Uncork the bottle, placing the thumb over the mouth. Cover the hole quickly. They never dig out. It costs less than four cents a hole.

SUFFOCATE YOUR WOODCHUCKS.

Being now in their burrows, woodchucks are helplessly in your power. Securely close all but one opening to the burrow, and down that roll a ball of rags saturated with "Fuma," Bisulfide of Carbon and quickly close the hole. H. C. B.

Three Rivers, Mass.

Rev. Wm. L. Palmer, from Norvell, Mich.

In order to be sure that Bisulfide of Carbon, which you manufacture, will kill Woodchucks after putting some of it into the hole and closing all the outlets, I waited about twenty-four hours, and then dug in and found them dead. This I have done twice, and I have no doubt of its efficacy, in every instance where the conditions are fulfilled. I will never be without it and will never be annoyed with that animal on the premises any longer.

WOODCHUCKS IN NEW HAMPSHIRE.

Woodchuck statistics, computed a few years ago by a New Hampshire student of economics, laid bare the fact that one healthy woodchuck—and there are no unhealthy woodchucks—would eat, and did eat, between the first of May and the first of September of any year, 500 pounds of red clover, first and second crops. An inside estimate placed the number of woodchucks then in New Hampshire at 482,960. No one made a business of hunting them, and if 10,000 were casually killed or trapped in a year that was a large number. The statistician, to be as easy as he could on the farmer, figured on the basis of 470,000 woodchucks in the State, all busy, during the four months mentioned, cutting and mowing away clover throughout New Hampshire—to say nothing of the other farm products they saved the farmer the trouble of gathering himself. If one woodchuck harvested 500 pounds of clover, of course there was no getting around the fact that, at the same rate, the 470,000 woodchucks gathered a crop of 235,000,000 pounds, the equivalent of 117,500 tons every year. Placing hay at even the ridiculous price of $6 a ton, here was the astounding exhibit, as plain as the simple rules of multiplication and division could make it, that the annual tribute woodchucks were levying on the hay fields of the patient New Hampshire farmer amounted to the sum of $705,000.

Petty larceny thief! That was the kind of petty larceny thief statistics proved the woodchuck to be in New Hampshire! And the one absorbing question in the state became, "How shall we suppress the woodchuck?" It had a leading place in politics that year, and when the legislature met, statesmanship took hold of it at once. A price was put on the head of this wholesale robber. Some eager legislators were in favor of offering 25 cents a head for woodchucks, but it was finally decided that the farmers would be satisfied to receive a bounty of 10 cents a woodchuck for running down these pests on their own farms, and 10 cents it was. From that moment the woodchuck became an outlaw in New Hampshire, and is so yet. The price put on his head wasn't a large one, but is such an inducement to hunt and trap the woodchuck that bounties on an average annual kill of 100,000 of the animals have been collected in this state ever since. The local statistician referred to calculates that this big removal of four-footed robbers has saved to the farmers not less than $125,000 annually on hay alone since the raids began.

But the actual number of woodchucks in New Hampshire seems to be as great as ever. This state is their paradise. How difficult it is to exterminate or to even keep within bounds the woodchuck when it has once colonized, may be imagined when, besides the protection the wily and cautious nature of this animal assures to it, the fact is known that the female brings forth two families a year, with from six to eight in each family. The young mature quickly and have families of their own before they are a year old.—New York Sun.

SURE DEATH TO WOODCHUCKS.

E. R. Taylor's "Fuma," that is, his "Bisulfide of Carbon," does kill woodchucks, for I have tried it twice to my satisfaction. I knew the animal was in the hole as I saw him go in. I took a round stone, nearly as large as a hen's egg, and rolled cotton batting around it, and turned into the batting about a tablespoonful of the liquid, and rolled that into the holes as far as I could. Then I stopped up all his holes perfectly tight, and left it for a day. Then I dug in to see if he was alive, and I found him dead as a stone. If you want to help farmers get rid of these pests, you can publish the above trials and proofs.

REV. WM. L. PALMER,
Jackson Co., Mich.

WOODCHUCKS OR GROUND HOGS, SHOULD THEY BE DESTROYED, AND HOW?

Yes, to be sure, kill the woodchucks. How? Use carbon bisulfide. My small farm was overrun with them, so I procured a can of the article, costing 45 cents for the pound, made balls of rags, of a size to go down into the holes, and after stopping all but one outlet, I saturated a ball and put it into the hole as far as I could reach and closed the hole airtight. The pound can made fifteen doses, and no woodchuck ever came out of his hole. If used after they have gone into winter quarters, a clean sweep can be made.

L. T. HADLEY,
So. Franklin, Mass.

Woodchucks are a great pest when allowed to multiply undisturbed. They destroy much grain by digging holes in the fields and throwing up mounds of earth, which are very annoying when working the land. They can be shot and trapped to some extent but there is a better way. Go to the druggist and get for 40 cents a pound bottle of bisulfide of carbon. Saturate a rag about six inches square with a tablespoonful of it, and with a stick shove the rag several feet into the hole. Then fill the mouth of the hole with earth. The inhabitants of each hole treated in this way will be destroyed.

R. C. TROWBRIDGE,
Tully, N. Y.

SQUIRRELS.

Pullman, Washington, May 25, 1895.

Mr. Edward R. Taylor, Cleveland, O.,

Dear Sir: I have found the carbon bisulfide sent this station by you to be highly effective in killing burrowing animals. Its advantages are that there is no danger of killing other animals as there is in the use of strychnine, or of setting fields on fire, as in the case in using phosphorus. It is also a positive remedy not depending on the squirrels. It seems to be a certain death to the squirrels, which are such a nuisance in this region. I am anxious to learn what the material can be sold for here at retail, as its advantages constrain me to recommend it above other methods in use here for exterminating squirrels.

Yours very truly,
W. J. SPEILMAN,
Agriculturist, State Experiment Station.

PRAIRIE DOG TOWN

PRAIRIE DOGS.

Please send me 100 lbs. of of your famous squirrel exterminator called "Fuma" Carbon Bisulfide. It has been used as an exterminator of the prairie dog here and has proven a great success.

J. M. ARCHULETA, JR.

Lumberton, New Mexico, April 12, 1895.

It is a sure shot. I have "swiped" about four thousand holes and they stay shut. I pronounce it the greatest dog exterminator on earth. R. E. BEATTY.

A STRONG ENDORSEMENT.

Edward R. Taylor, Esq.; Cleveland, O.

DEAR SIR:—I have seen an article in regard to destroying prairie dogs, etc., with your "Fuma." I can testify to its good qualities, having used it myself with some neighbors during the summer of 1890, most effectually in exterminating them from at least 800 acres. I used cotton batting, making a piece not larger than an egg. My experience has been that it is death to all the dogs in the hole, whether one or a dozen. Yours truly,

JOHN B. T., Helena, Mont.

MOSES MARSHALL, Ames, Kans., writes:—"Your Bisulfide of Carbon killed all the Prairie Dogs on my farm;" and ISAIAH LIGHTNER says:—"I have destroyed all my dogs on eighty acres at a cost of thirty dollars, and increased the value of the land five hundred dollars. No humbug about it."

TREATING BUSHES AND TREES.

In treating currant bushes, gooseberry trees, raspberries, strawberries, tomatoes and other growing plants: Construct a small bell-shaped tent, with iron hoops or canes, and upon this frame fasten oiled canvas or thick paper; fix a wire hook to hang from the top of the frame inside, pouring a small quantity of the bisulphide into a little toy bucket hung from this. With the handles at each side the tent can be carried along and placed over the bushes or plants. The tent should be made so it will fit close to the ground, and if carefully lifted from plant to plant there need be but little waste of liquid. The tent should remain over the trees for five, ten or fifteen minutes; a great many subjects can be treated in a short time, and all insects, caterpillars, grubs, worms, larvae, etc., destroyed.

G. M. S.

KEEPING RATS OUT OF SEED POTATO CELLARS.

To protect our stock from rats we use in our cellars Taylor's Bisulfide of Carbon, furnished by Edward R. Taylor, Cleveland, O. No vermin can live where its fumes penetrate, and as the vapor is much heavier than air it follows the runways and drives the rats away.

From Farmer's Bulletin, 297.
FUMIGATION.

Rats may be destroyed in their burrows in the fields, and, still more important, in levees and rice-field dikes, by the use of carbon bisulphid. A wad of cotton or other absorbent material is saturated with the liquid and pushed into the burrow, the opening being packed with soil to prevent escape of the gas. All animals in the burrow are asphyxiated. Fumigation about buildings is not so effective, as the gas cannot readily be confined.

HOW TO DESTROY WORMS IN CHESTNUTS.

The two species of chestnut weevil known in North America infest the chestnuts and chinquapins in every locality where the latter grow naturally. Three methods of combating these enemies seem to me practical:

First, gather the nuts as they fall, and as soon as enough are on hand to warrant treatment, put them in a tight barrel, box or other receptacle that can be tightly covered. Procure a half pint or more of bisulphide of carbon, and pour some in an open cup which should be placed with the nuts. It will permeate every space, and kill all the larvae and eggs within 36 hours, if securely confined. It will not injure the nuts either for eating or planting if they are not longer subjected to treatment and are afterwards well aired. However, there is no danger from poisoning, except by inhaling the fumes. No fire should be allowed near, as the gas is very inflammable.—From Rural New Yorker.

DEATH TO PRAIRIE DOGS.

Editor Journal, Columbus, Neb.,

Dear Sir:—It was my fortune in purchasing land here in Platte county to have a few prairie dogs thrown in, as a nuisance, and it has ever since been my wish to get rid of them. I tried various kinds of poison, shooting, drowning, etc., but all failed until quite recently I learned that bisulphide of carbon would destroy them. It is a liquid, can be purchased at a drug store at a cost of from 10 to 15 cents a pound by the quantity. I bought from three different parties; the best and cheapest I got from Edward R. Taylor, of Cleveland, Ohio. It is sure death to prairie dogs, gophers, squirrels, etc. Mode of applying it: Take a piece of cotton the size of a hen's egg, saturate it with about one-half an ounce of the Bisulphide of Carbon, throw it into the hole of the animal, cover the top of hole with ground, so that the cotton is loose in the hole. A gas is formed and the dogs are killed. I have destroyed my dogs on about 80 acres at a cost of $30.00, and increased the value of the land $500.00. One pound will do for 25 holes. This medicine is quickly applied and is sure death. No humbug about it.

Very respectfully thy friend,
ISAIAH LIGHTNER,

Matson, Platte county, Neb.

Bisulphide of Carbon is sure death to all burrowing animals. Also one-half ounce to the ton of grain in a close bin, will kill all weevils or other insects therein without the least harm to the grain.

THE APPLE MAGGOT "TRYPETA POMONELLA."

Answered by Prof. M. V. Slingerland, in Rural New Yorker, April 20, 1895.

Is it practicable to use Carbon Bisulfide to destroy the maggots and eggs in freshly gathered apples? Can it be used effectively against the insect in the pupæ state?

Yes, if you can place the fruit in a practically air tight receptacle, and place the Carbon Bisulfide in shallow dishes on top of the fruit, using about one pound of the liquid to one ton of the fruit, and leaving it for several hours, I believe that it will kill all insect life in the fruit. It would thus be practicable to destroy the insects in any stage in the stored fruit; but this will only be partially effective in eradicating the pest, because thousands of maggots went into the ground from the windfalls. Combine the two methods of keeping the windfalls picked up clean, and treating the gathered fruit with the Carbon Bisulfide, and you cannot help but greatly check the pest.

Yes, the Carbon Bisulfide will kill the pupæ that may have been formed, either in the fruit or on the bottom of the barrel or bin

STAVE BORERS.

Pomona, Florida, Dec. 10, 1895.

E. R. Taylor, Esq.,

Dear Sir: The 50 lbs. of "Fuma" which I ordered from you reached here 7th November. The following day I put it into "watering pots" and had it sprinkled over all the casks in my wine-cellar. Then there was left about a gallon which I left standing in an open vessel on the cellar floor, then closed the doors and left for the Atlanta Exposition, where we remained for two weeks. During this time the cellar was not opened.

On my return I found the odor of the Fuma yet pervading the cellar; the casks were covered with tiny crystals, which sparkled like diamonds and every stave borer killed. In short, the result of the experiment proved entirly satisfactory in every way. I herewith inclose my check on N. Y. for $5.00 in payment. Yours truly,

HOLMES ERWIN.

NEW USE FOR BISULPHIDE OF CARBON.

A new use for bisulphide of carbon has been discovered which ought to make it very popular and of large consumption. The peculiar and highly inflammable gas evolved from this powerful and volatile fluid has a downward as well as an upward tendency, a circumstance which renders its use for the destruction of weevils, insects of all kinds, vermin, etc., of the highest practical utility.

An experiment was recently made in the following manner: A small bottle of the fluid, about one pound, was placed on the floor of an empty 1,000 bushel bin, with a small piece of muslin cloth placed loosely on top of the bottle instead of a cork; over all was placed a broken box so as to protect the bottle from being upset or broken, and then the bin was filled to its utmost capacity with corn. On top of the pile another bottle was placed, having the same arrangement as the one buried beneath the grain.

The result was highly satisfactory. The live weevils admitted from the field while housing the grain were utterly destroyed and none further appeared.

CARBON BISULFIDE FOR CRAWFISH.

Howard Evarts Weed, before the Association of Economic Entomologists, Springfield, Mass., August 28, 1895.

Crawfish sometimes do much injury to corn and other crops in land that contains considerable moisture, through a lack of proper drainage. In some fields their holes are so numerous that they average in number nearly nine to the square foot, and on such land, of course it would be impossible to raise any cultivated crop. Such fields are generally abandoned and only broomsedge and a few of the coarser grasses will grow on land of this description. Crawfish are also numerous along the bottom and sides of open ditches, and, by their work along the levees of the Mississippi river, they cause weak places in the embankment through which the water gets a little start. Once let the water get started in this way the opening is gradually washed larger; soon the embankment gives way, and an overflow is the result.

Such being the damage done by these pests, the question of how to destroy them becomes of no small importance, and perhaps some experiments of mine in this direction may be of interest. In the spring of 1903 I noticed that the bottom of a wide, open ditch near the Experiment Station building was lined with crawfish holes. Having doubts as to whether or no carbon bisulfide would kill the crawfish, I poured an ounce of bisulfide in each hole, closing the hole immediately with the foot by pressing the surrounding dirt together. A stick was placed by the side of where each hole had been, so as to be able to tell if the same holes were reopened or if new ones were made. The ditch was examined every day for some time, but none of the holes were reopened, showing that the bisulfide had been effective. No new holes were made along the ditch for three weeks, and then only two, which were probably made by some newcomers.

Upon two occasions the crawfish have been dug out the day after the bisulfide treatment, when it was found that they had been killed. Their holes may be anywhere from one to fifteen feet or more deep. They dig deep enough to get to water, and in wet weather, or on low places, their holes are not so deep as in dry weather or on higher places. For two years past it has been a common practice with me to treat crawfish holes with bisulfide, and in every case, with but one exception, the treatment has been successful.

The particulars of this exception are as follows: In September, 1893, a place on rather high, but poorly drained land on the college campus, was graded and put in shape for a tennis court. The ground being somewhat sloping, about three feet was taken from one end and added to the other end, in order to make it level. A few days after the court was fixed, many crawfish holes were noticed, both upon the end where the dirt had been added and where it had been taken away. These holes were treated in the usual manner with carbon bisulfide, fully expecting this treatment would rid the tennis court of the crawfish. The next day, however, it was found that the holes had been reopened during the night, and a second treatment was made, using fully double the amount of the carbon bisulfide. The result of the carbon bisulfide being the same as the first, daily treatments were then made for over two weeks, in some cases nearly a pound of bisulfide being used. It was fully three months before the tennis court was free from the crawfish, but whether they left the ground for a more favorable situation, or were killed, I am not prepared to say. Bisulfide from the same can was effective in other places, so that the cause of failure was not due to the quality of the bisulfide used.

Were it not for this one case of the failure of the carbon bisulfide to do effective work, I would be prepared to recommend it for crawfish in all cases. The failure mentioned, however, was under somewhat unnatural conditions, and as we have used it at the station successfully over fifty times, with but this one case of failure, it may be said that the carbon bisulfide is nearly, if not quite, a complete remedy for crawfish. On land where they are so numerous it will not always pay to treat them in the manner described, as the treatment would cost nearly as much as the land. But in the garden and along the levees of the Mississippi river, there is no question but that the treatment would pay.

ANTS.

Mr. R. E. Beatty, of Deer Trail, Colorado, writes as follows to the *Field and Farm* of Denver:

"To kill red ants, pour two tablespoonfuls of Bisulfide of Carbon in their main entrance. Some light the gas and explode it, and say it works better, but I find the quickest way is to take an iron bar and make a hole down through the middle two feet deep, then pour in some of the liquid and close the hole, and it will make a clean sweep."

H. & Co., Clifton, Arizona, say: "Your Bisulfide of Carbon, is a sure deaduer on red ants."

ALFALFA, GOPHERS AND MOLES.

How to Cultivate the One, and also How to Exterminate the Others.

A subscriber from Parsons, Kansas, wishes information on the following points: Is alfalfa a clover? Is it any more beneficial to the soil than red clover? Is it any more nutritious in a green state than the clovers? Is it more nutritious than hay? Will the red clover succeed under the same treatment as alfalfa where irrigation is necessary?

Another correspondent from Wamego, Kansas, wishes to know what is the best mode of fighting gophers and moles, which he states are the pests of the alfalfa field, especially on the alluvial soils of the river bottoms. He states that for more than ten years he has been growing alfalfa in his section, has cut as much as five tons per acre, and, in some seasons, twenty-one tons on three acres, but that the stand has always been ruined after three or four years and the land had to be changed, and he therefore wishes to know the best method of destroying the gophers or moles in the alfalfa field. He states that his boys have trapped them by the hundred, but that they multiply in spite of all efforts at extermination.

It is evident from communications like the above, says the *Iowa Homestead*, that there is a widespread interest on the subject of alfalfa growing, and therefore, we answer these questions somewhat in detail. Alfalfa is not, strictly speaking, a clover. It is a legume, and hence both belong to the same family and are closely related. They are, however, adapted to different conditions, and we know of no place where both are first-class crops under the same conditions. It may be stated as a maxim that clover ends where alfalfa begins, and where they are both grown side by side on precisely the same soil, neither of them do their best. Clover is partial to a clay soil, although it does not do its best in heavy clays because of its liability to heave out during the freezing and thawing of the spring. Alfalfa does best on an alluvial or other light soil with a permanent supply of water underneath, where it is not supplied by irrigation, and with no intervening stratum of clay or coarse gravel between the surface and the water. Both of them supply nitrogen to the soil by means of the bacteria that lives on the nodules of their roots; so do beans, peas, locust trees, and in fact all other legumes. Alfalfa has a higher nutritive ration than red clover, and hence is more valuable for stock that is fed largely on corn or the non-saccharine sorghums. Whether or not it is more nutritious than hay depends upon how each are cured. When both are cured equally well alfalfa hay is the superior. The clovers will succeed under irrigation, but under these circumstances it is much more profitable to grow the alfalfa.

Where a farmer is growing alfalfa or clover, and especially in a country where these are not generally grown, he will find he has to feed about all the gophers and moles in the country. They know enough to leave tough prairie grass roots and go where they can find something better. There is no way to avoid this. The only way is to kill them. As our correspondent states, trapping is slow work. The Idaho agricultural experiment station has issued bulletin No. 4, covering this ground, and the conclusion to which they arrive is that Carbon Bisulfide is the best exterminator of moles, gophers, squirrels, and all this class of vermin. Prof. E. W. Hillgard, of the University of California, where squirrels are very plentiful and destructive, has also experimented with Carbon Bisulfide, in fact, originated that method of treatment, and in his hands it has proven a cheap, safe, and reliable remedy. It has also been tried on a number of farms and ranches in different parts of Idaho and Washington, and the results are eminently satisfactory. The method of using it is to pour some of it on balls of horse dung, which seems to be the best and most approved medium, and place it, late in the evening, in their burrows, closing the entrance at once. The best results are secured by using what is known as Fuma Carbon Bisulfide, manufactured by E. R. Taylor, manufacturing chemist. The chemical will cost but one cent a hole, and the total cost, including labor, should not be far over two cents a hole. Extreme care must be taken in using it not to let fire in any form get near the vapor as it is very highly inflammable. It is heavier than air, and when used as above, and the hole covered up, fills the hole with vapor which means death to whatever is found in it. Many farmers in the State of Washington have used it on tracts of a thousand acres and with success. Mr. W. N. Ruby, of Colfax, Washington, reported to the Idaho station that he had saved from fifteen to twenty thousand bushels of wheat by the use of $150.00 worth of chemicals.

FUMIGATION WITH BISULFIDE OF CARBON FOR THE COMPLETE AND RAPID DESTRUCTION OF THE INSECTS WHICH ATTACK HERBARIUM SPECIMENS, FURS, WOOLENS, ETC.

By H. DU BUYSSON, Broût, Vernet, France.

Insect Life, Vol. VI., No. 2, Pages 159, 160, 161.

The fumigating chest for use with Bisulfide of Carbon has been employed for many years in the preservation of unpoisoned herbaria, which would infallibly be devoured without this annual or biennial precaution. These fumigations may render great service in the preservation of other objects more useful than the specimens of a herbarium. I shall describe, therefore, the first method used, and every one will know how to apply it to his own needs.

DESCRIPTION OF THE FUMIGATING CHEST.

It is in principle a rectangular box of light wood, lined with thin zinc, which is carefully soldered at all joints. Around the edge of the box, inside, runs a little gutter of zinc, carefully soldered. This gutter is filled with water and serves to make a water seal by means of the flange of the lid, which is also covered with zinc and carries all around a strip of the metal bent at right angles, and long enough to plunge into the water in the gutter. In this way the box is hermetically sealed and the vapors of the Bisulfide cannot possibly escape from it.

USE IN THE PRESERVATION OF HERBARIA.

Botanists now generally poison their specimens, and the fumigating box is seldom used. Nevertheless it has served me well and I still resort to it from time to time, to preserve such plants as I have not time to submit to the action of arsenic in alcohol or to bichloride of mercury.

The process in question is based upon the great volatility of Bisulfide of carbon at ordinary pressure and moderate temperature. The penetration of its vapor is so considerable that we have only to pile up in the chest the mounting sheets of the herbarium, one above the other, in order to fumigate them. They are penetrated to the very center and eggs, larva, and perfect insects. Anobium or Attagenus, are killed. Space should be left and right of the pile for the vessels containing the Bisulfide. Those which I use are of zinc and measure 10cm. long, 6cm. wide, and 9cm. deep. There is no risk in prolonging the fumigation; on the contrary there is but the greater certainty of its being efficacious. Five or six days will be time enough. No limit need be set to the quantity of Bisulfide used; what is not evaporated will serve for a new charge.

The disagreeable odor of Bisulfide of carbon is not persistent; it is not even necessary to spread open the mounting sheets; it is only necessary to expose them, unopened, to the air. I would call attention, however, to one very necessary precaution, if accidents are to be avoided. The vapor of Bisulfide is very inflammable, and the chest must, therefore, be set in a safe place and not opened near a fire or any flame whatever. It would be risky, for example, to unpack the chest in the evening while holding a lamp in the hand.

As the odor of Bisulfide is very disagreeable, and may cause discomfort to some persons, all these operations should be performed in an attic or in an apartment of which the windows may be left open as long as necessary.

PRESERVATION OF FURS AND WOOLENS.

The same process may be used in the preservation of clothing in clothing establishments, civil or military, where Tinea and Attagenus sometimes cause such ravages. Special arrangements may be adopted in establishing fumigating chests or rooms to avoid the settling due to weight and to facilitate the penetration of the gas.

This method makes it certain that we shall not "shut the wolf up in the sheepfold." Articles fumigated are entirely rid of eggs, larvæ, and living insects. They may be shaken out in the open air for greater security and then replaced on the shelves, with the assurance that they will not be found gnawed when next visited.

PRESERVATION OF THE STUFFING OF FURNITURE AND SADDLES.

Tinea and Attagenus have a marked predilection for horsehair, so that these insects are sometimes found flourishing in the stuffing of our furniture, even that which is in daily use. This process has the advantage of permitting us to destroy them without having recourse to the upholsterer; we need but to construct a fumigating chest large enough to contain a couple of armchairs or more. In the same way we may treat mattresses, eiderdown quilts, or anything which is supposed to contain eggs or larvæ.

I have experimented with a saddle much damaged by moths, and after fumigating it five days noticed no appearance of insects; the saddle was completely penetrated by the vapor and all the moths perished. I kept it two years under observation in order to be assured of the efficacy of the process.

DISINFECTION IN EPIDEMICS.

I am persuaded that clothing subjected to this process would be disinfected quite as well as by the processes usually employed in certain epidemics, such as typhus, cholera, smallpox, etc. It seems to me that the vapors which penetrate fabrics so well and kill insects so thoroughly would act in the same way upon the microbes which engender epidemics.*

In discussing this paper Mr. Atkinson stated that he had used a very similar box in fumigating objects infected with insects.

Mr. Garman calls attention to the fact that at the museum of comparative zoology at Cambridge a large upright zinc-lined case was constantly used for disinfecting the skins of birds and mammals.

Mr. Riley had used Bisulfide of Carbon successfully for his insect collection.

Mr. Smith had used it successfully for ants, and found it not injurious to vegetation.

Mr. Garman reported having found it effective in destroying the melon louse. His method of applying it was to roll the vines up in a heap, then invert a tub over them, and after placing a saucer containing a tablespoonful of Bisulfide under the tub its edges were pressed down into the soil or the earth was drawn up when necessary. He had tried the fumes of burning sulphur and tobacco, but the former injured the plants and the latter did not kill the plant lice, many of them gradually recovering after being stupefied by it.

Mr. Smith thought since the aphides often spread from particular plants or hills, the use of Bisulfide in good season might make it possible to prevent the injuries of these insects. (See next page.)

* NOTE. I have observed in Bisulfide of Carbon no clearly defined power of taking out the colors of fabrics which I have subjected to its vapors. It may, therefore, be used without fear, except, perhaps, in the case of the most delicate tints.

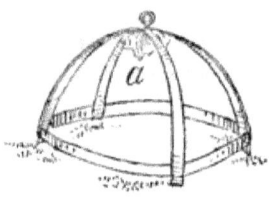

A FUMATORIUM.

Would it not be a good plan for every florist and seedsman to have constructed an air-tight building into which could be placed manure or soil for the greenhouse benches or potting; also flower pots, rustic vases, pot plants, flowering shrubs, etc.; these could all be treated by the fumes of bisulphide of carbon. For every ton of manure or soil, one pound of the liquid placed in a basin or saucer will be sufficient. Leave the place closed for two or three days, according to quantity of material. Pot plants, etc., can be treated with a proportionate amount, according to quantity of plants.

See page 30.

A Homemade Cover for Fumigation with Bisulfide of Carbon.

[*From Insect Life, No. 4, Vol. VII, p. 355.*]

Mr. Edward R. Taylor of Cleveland, Ohio, in a recent letter suggests the following method of making a cheap cover for use in fumigating low-growing plants with Bisulfide of Carbon:

Take a barrel hoop, cut it in two, and fasten the pieces at right angles to each other, by making a hole with a brad awl through both and inserting a screw eye with the eye on the convex side, to be used as a handle for lifting. Spring the hoops to make a cover of the size wanted, notch the ends, and tie a string around, as in making a kite; or better use a stiff wire or a full hoop. Take manilla or even newspaper, cover all of one side with paste, and cover one section (one-fourth of the "dome") with it, turning all the surplus paper inside. The other three sections are covered with paper in the same way, turning the surplus paper either inside or outside, as it would naturally go. A bundle of rags or cotton can be tied inside where the hoops cross to receive the charge of Bisulfide. Any of the chemical left after treating one hill can be carried with little loss to the next. This will make a more substantial cover than one would at first think, even when made of newspapers, as when dry the paste will make them very stiff, especially when there are several thicknesses of paper. The covers will also be very resistant to the vapors of the Bisulfide of Carbon.

The Treatment of Greenhouse Plants with Bisulfide of Carbon for the Destruction of Red Spider and Aphides.

[*From Am. Florist.*]

From the fact that some field experiments with Bisulfide of Carbon, have yielded encouraging results in the treatment of Cucurbs for the destruction of aphides, it appeared not improbable that the same agent might be employed for a similar purpose in the greenhouse.

The Carbon was introduced through a stationary glass tube inserted in a hole in the top of the box, the lower end of this tube being provided with a sponge to retain the Carbon while it was evaporating, the upper end being closed with a cork stopper in order to retain the fumes.

With pelargoniums infested by aphides, one-half dram Carbon Bisulfide, for three hours, was found to be thoroughly effective in destroying the insects without injury to the plants. Chrysanthemums infested with the ordinary brown aphis so common on these plants, were treated with one dram for two hours; this destroyed the insects without affecting the plants, which were in this case tender shoots brought directly from the cellar in which they were being wintered, and would therefore probably be more susceptible to injury. Cinerarias were treated in precisely the same manner also for aphides, and with both these and the chrysanthemums, the experiment seemed an unqualified success.

The accompanying illustration shows the complete box as used to enclose large potted plants. It would seem that this method of treatment admits of application to a greater or less degree, according to circumstances. The results indicate very little danger to ordinary greenhouse plants from the use of the vapor of Carbon Bisulfide. We were assisted in these experiments by Mr. W. A. Porter, and the tests were made in the greenhouses of the Ohio Agricultural Experiment Station.

F. M. WEBSTER, Entomologist,
AUG. D. SELBY, Botanist

Wooster, Ohio, March 1, 1895.

BISULFIDE OF CARBON AS AN INSECTICIDE.

Reprinted from Insect Life, Vol. 7, No. 2, page 108. U. S. Dept. of Agriculture.

At the late meeting of the Association of the Economic Entomologists, in August, 1894, at Brooklyn, N. Y., Prof. J. B. Smith, of New Jersey. read a paper on this subject. He referred to its limited use for many years. He had become interested in Prof. Garman's experiments in destroying aphides infesting melon vines, and began experiments for himself. On pot-grown plants, he found that it killed the lice, but if used in large quantities, killed the plants also. The appearance of lice on cantaloupe and melon vines furnished him the opportunity he desired for experiment. He says :

I procured a dozen wooden bowls thirteen inches in diameter and six inches deep, inside measurement, and a series of small, graduated tumblers, in which "1 teaspoonful" and "1 dram" corresponded. To get at the rate of evaporation I poured one dram into a graduate and left it exposed, but placed in a shaded spot. It required fifteen minutes to disappear completely. Eleven badly infested hills were then covered by bowls, the vines being crowded under when necessary, and 1 dram in a graduate was placed under each. At the end of twenty minutes I lifted one bowl, found that less than half the material had evaporated; that all the Coccinellidæ were dead, the small lice dying, and the Diabrotica, ants, and large viviparous aphides were yet all alive. Ten minutes later there was little change. At the end of three-fourths of an hour, though scarcely more than half the liquid was gone, all save a few of the mature, wingless, viviparous females were dead. In one hour there was yet liquid in all the graduates ; but all the aphides were dead, or appeared so. To test the matter, all the hills treated were marked to be examined later. Another series of infested hills was selected ; but the experiment was varied by using 2 drams of Bisulfide in some cases, using a shallow saucer in others, pouring the liquid on the ground in two cases, and covering other hills with large, square boxes, some of them anything but tight. All coverings were left on for one hour undisturbed. Examined first a square box covering a shallow saucer with 2 drams of Bisulfide; found this all evaporated and every aphis killed. The bowls covering the saucers in which 1 dram was used showed like results. Two square boxes which were not tight, covering graduates with 2 drams of liquid, had all insects unaffected and the material scarcely half gone. The two bowls under which the Bisulfide was poured on the ground were then lifted and all the aphides were found dead. All the other hills covered by bowls showed all the lice dead and not all the Bisulfide evaporated. The hills first treated were again examined and there was no sign of recovered life anywhere visible. Bowls, graduates, and Bisulfide were left with Mr. Taylor, and all the treated hills were marked for later examination and to note the effects of the chemical. The experiments were made in the middle of a very hot day, the thermometer 93° in the shade, little or no wind blowing, and the sand so hot that it burned through shoe soles and could scarcely be handled more than a few moments at a time. Many of the hills showed the edges of the leaves, when the covers removed, yellowed and set with numerous drops of a clear liquid. I feared permanent injury, but instructed Mr. Taylor if he found that the plants died to continue his work before the sun was high or after it was quite low. He wrote me under date of July 19: "The hills you treated when here last started to grow nicely, except the two hills where the Carbon was poured on the ground; that killed them. The treated hills showed no lice at last examination." I am quite satisfied from the experiments above recorded and from others that were not recorded, but were simply made to settle practical questions, that in melon fields at least Bisulfide of Carbon can be used satisfactorily and effectively. It has the enormous advantage of reaching everything on all parts of the plant, not a specimen escaping. With a stock of from 50 to 100 light covering-boxes about 18 inches in diameter, as many shallow dishes, and a bottle of Bisulfide, the infested hills in a field can be treated in a comparatively short time.

The discussion that followed this paper brought out the virtues of Bisulfide of Carbon in a clear light. Mr. Davis reported its use in Michigan to destroy woodchucks. Peas and beans exposed to the vapor for two hours were effectually rid of the "bugs" that infest them. Stored grain infested with weevil was cleared of the pest by pouring over the surface an ounce of Bisulfide to 100 pounds of grain. Melon vines could be confined under a washtub or any other close vessel, and get rid of lice, etc., in a few hours. When plants are small, a small vessel only is required—something to confine the vapor.

Mr. Southwick coincided with the author of the paper in the importance and value of prompt preventive measures, and stated that he was especially interested in the use of Bisulfide of Carbon, which he had employed in his work in Central Park since 1884. He referred to a new wash, a combination of Bisulfide with "polysolve," which he used in the form of an emulsion. He stated, however, that "polysolve" was no longer being manufactured, but thought its place might be taken by kerosene emulsion.

THE WOOD LEOPARD MOTH, OR IMPORTED ELM BORER.

(ZEUZERA PYRINA, L.)

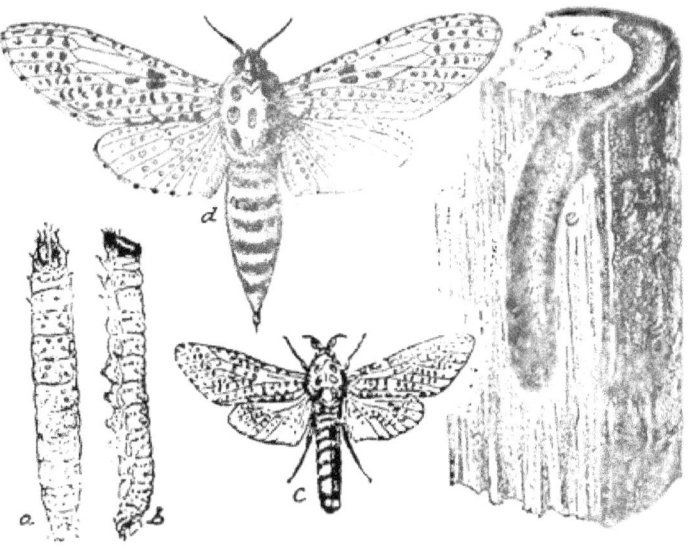

FIG. 2.

The wood leopard moth; *a, b*, larva from above and from side; *c*, male moth; *d*, female moth; *e*, larval burrow. All natural size.

[*From Insect Life, Vol. 6, p. 61.*]

Mr. E. B. Southwick, Entomologist to the New York Park Commissioners, says that this is the most troublesome of all the insects infesting the New York City parks. Wagon-loads of twigs and branches are trimmed off in Central Park annually, and the insect seems now to have been somewhat checked. The openings to the burrows made by the larvæ are easily seen by the trained eye, and where they are in the trunks of valuable trees or shrubs, or in branches that cannot be easily spared, a few drops of Bisulfide of Carbon are forced into the burrow by means of an ordinary oil can holding half a pint, such as is used by mechanics, and a little dab of putty closes the opening. The vapor of the Bisulfide will penetrate the full length of the tunnel, and will kill the larva wherever it may be in it, without injury to the tree.

THE SQUASH BUG.

ANASA TRISTIS, DEGEER.

[Abstract from Bulletin 75, New York Ag. Exp. Station, Geneva, N. Y.]

The squash-bug is probably very well known to most Long Island farmers; as it has been unusually abundant on all parts of the Island for several years past and especially during the past season. Indeed, it is safe to say that this insect is known to almost every one for it may be found at any time of the year, either sucking the sap from the vines in the garden or hidden away during the winter months under some board or in the wood pile or beneath almost any rubbish that will afford protection from the cold winter winds. The full grown bug is about five-eighths of an inch long, blackish-brown in color above and dull ochre-yellow beneath. When roughly handled or suddenly disturbed it emits a disgusting odor which has given it the rather undignified name of "stink bug."

This insect is an old and well known pest to growers of squashes and other cucurbits. It is found throughout the United States, and when occurring in large numbers is to be much dreaded. In some localities on Long Island its work is considered at times to be almost as serious as that of the squash-vine borer. Its ravages on the Island this past year, especially in the vicinity of Jamaica and Brooklyn, have been unusually severe. In this locality squashes are grown in abundance, forming one of the main crops.

The squash-bug belongs to one of the largest orders of insects which includes more than ten thousand species found in the United States. To this group belong many of our most serious insect pests, including the plant lice and scale insects. They are known as true bugs, and are designated by the term *Hemiptera*. The *Hemiptera* are partially characterized by the mouth parts being modified so as to form a more or less slender beak by means of which the tissue of the host is punctured and the liquid on which they feed is sucked from beneath. Fig. 6, plate I, is a side view of the head and beak of a squash-bug. When at rest the beak is drawn up and lies along the underside of the head and thorax.

Although usually preferring squash vines this insect is not infrequently found attacking melon and pumpkin vines. The bugs puncture the tissue with their stout beaks, inject a drop of poisonous saliva and suck the sap. The poison causes the tissue in the vicinity of the puncture to wilt and finally die, thus causing much more harm than the mere loss of sap. Nearly all parts of the plant are liable to attack. Even the fruit does not escape, and the bugs are frequently found, on young vines especially, attacking the roots just below the surface of the ground.

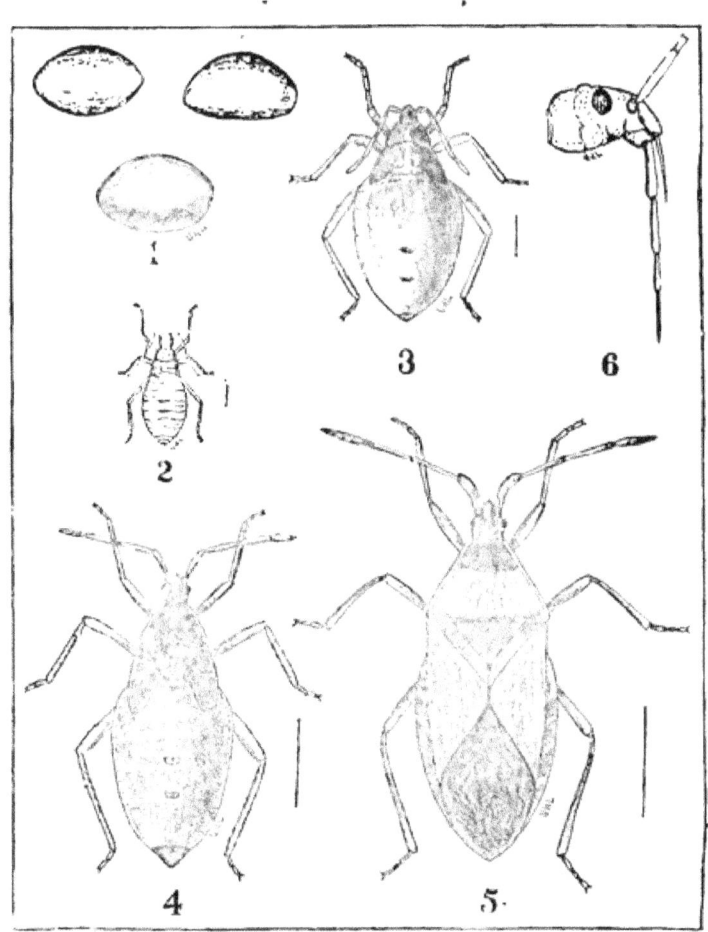

PLATE I.—THE SQUASH BUG.

1.—Eggs; greatly enlarged. 2.—Young bug, after second molt. 3 and 4.—Same, more fully developed. 5.—Adult. 6.—Head and beak, side view. Enlarged. (Original.)

REMEDIES.

"An ounce of prevention is worth a pound of cure," in this case especially, for when squash bugs once get well started in a field it is almost impossible to get rid of them. Insecticides are as a rule of but little value. Poisons would be of no use as the insect does not bite the tissue but sucks the sap from beneath. There are few odors more offensive than that emitted by this "old timer sinner," and a repellant that would drive a more respectable bug away will have little or no effect upon this one. So far as has been observed, those farmers on Long Island who have succeeded best in combating this pest are those who do not allow any rubbish to accumulate on or near their squash fields. Clean culture is always embarassing to the squash-bug.

Several farmers have asked with regard to the value of kerosene emulsion, insect powder, etc., as a remedy for the squash bug. As before stated, insecticides and repellants are generally considered of but little value in this case. However, the following account of experiments and observations may be of interest:

Early in September a field of squashes in the vicinity of Brooklyn was found to be badly infested by this insect.

Owing to the great number of insects present and the different stages represented, this field furnished a very good opportunity for testing the effect of Bisulfide of Carbon. Accordingly two fluid ounces of the Carbon were poured into a shallow dish and placed near a fallen and withered leaf upon which were numerous squash bugs of all sizes. A large sheet-iron bucket, which happened to be near at hand, about three feet across the top, was inverted over the whole and the edges forced into the ground to prevent the circulation of air. At the end of half an hour the bucket was removed and about fifty bugs which were nearest the dish were apparently dead. Twenty-five of them, the older ones, revived soon after being exposed to the air. The Carbon was only partially evaporated. Subsequent experiments, both in the field and laboratory, showed that a much less amount of Carbon is sufficient but that the insects should be exposed for a much longer time. The young bugs are much more susceptible than the mature insects. The weather was cool with a stiff breeze blowing. On a warm day the liquid would have evaporated more rapidly and thus been more effective.

The Bisulfide of Carbon could be applied in the spring when the young vines are being attacked by the newly hatched insects. Any tight covering sufficiently large to cover the vines should be placed over the hill and a very little Bisulfide in a shallow dish placed under it and allowed to remain for an hour or two. It is hoped that some experiments of this kind may be tried in the spring.

When confined under a tight covering and exposed to Bisulfide of carbon, squash-bugs are killed by it. Young bugs, those less than half grown, are much more susceptible than mature ones.

PLATE II.—SQUASH BUGS ON WITHERED LEAF.
(From Photograph.)

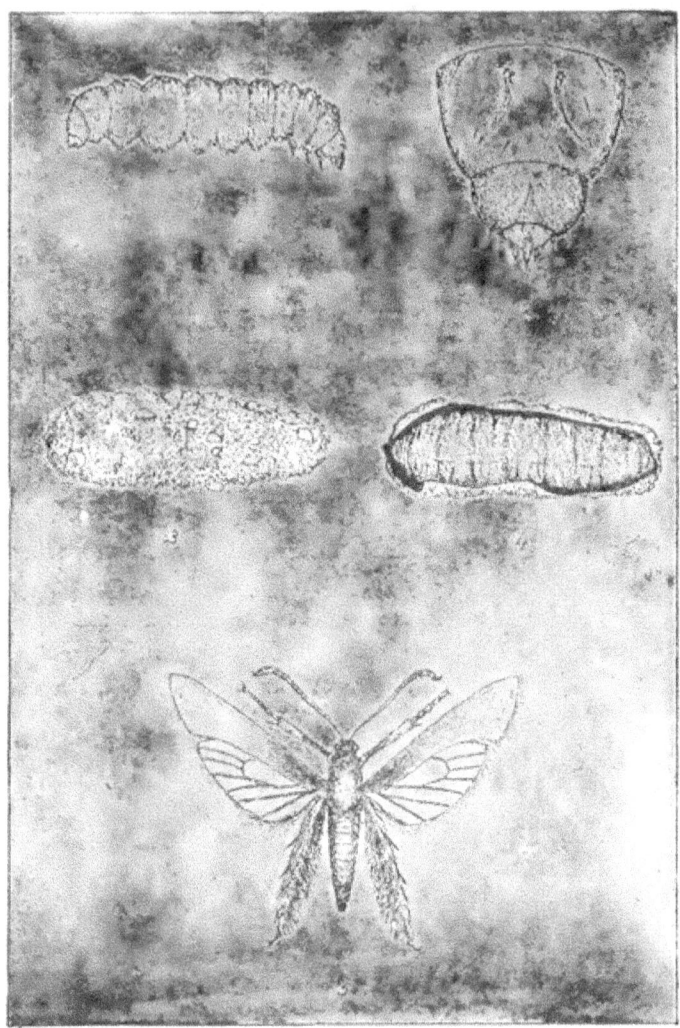

PLATE III.—THE SQUASH VINE BORER.

Fig. 1.—Larva. 2.—Head and first segment, showing V-shaped marking. 3.—Cocoon in which larva passes the winter. 4.—Same cut open, showing larva. All enlarged about one-half, with the exception of Fig. 2, which is greatly enlarged. (Original.)

CARBON BISULFIDE FOR CABBAGE ROOT MAGGOT.

[*From Bulletin 78, New York Agricultural Experiment Station, Ithaca, N. Y. Prof. M. V. Slingerland.*]

Prof. Cook was the first to experiment with this volatile substance on the root maggots. In 1880, he used it for this purpose "with the happiest results. A small hole was made in the earth near the main root of the plant, by the use of a walking stick, and about 15 cubic centimeters of the liquid poured in, and the hole quickly filled with earth, which was pressed down with the foot. In every case the insects were killed without injury to the plants." The next year, Prof. Cook found that its use was not practicable in radish

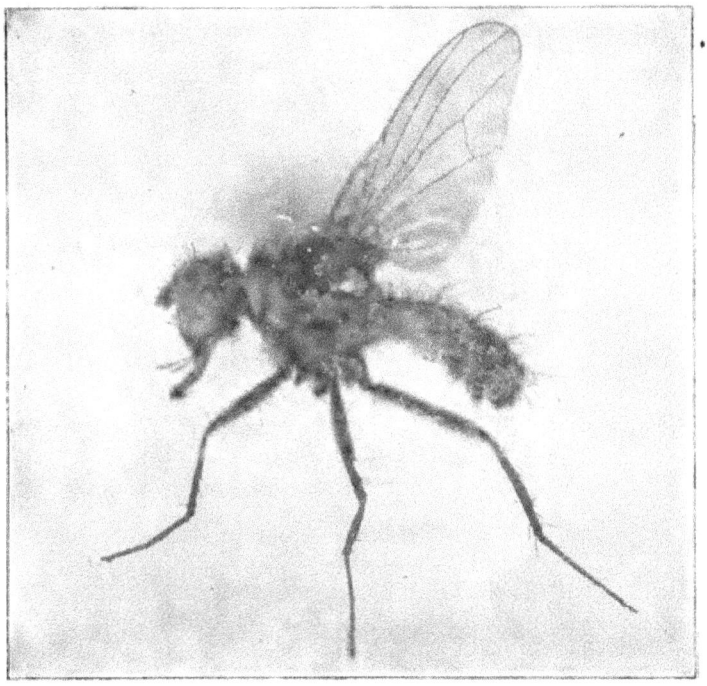

Fig. 4.—The male fly, side view with right legs and wing removed, greatly enlarged; natural length of the body represented by the white hair line below.

beds owing to the great number of plants to be treated, thus requiring so much liquid as to make it an expensive treatment; he tried making a few applications at short distances apart in the bed, but not with satisfactory results. In 1884, some of Prof. Cook's correspondents reported that the substance sometimes injured the cabbage plants, and its efficiency varied with the nature of the soil. The same year, Mr. Goff "found that Bisulfide of Carbon applied to the soil about the roots of radishes, destroyed the maggots that had not yet entered the root, but it had no perceptible effect upon those within."

Fig. 5—Female fly, similar view and magnification as the male fly in fig. 4.

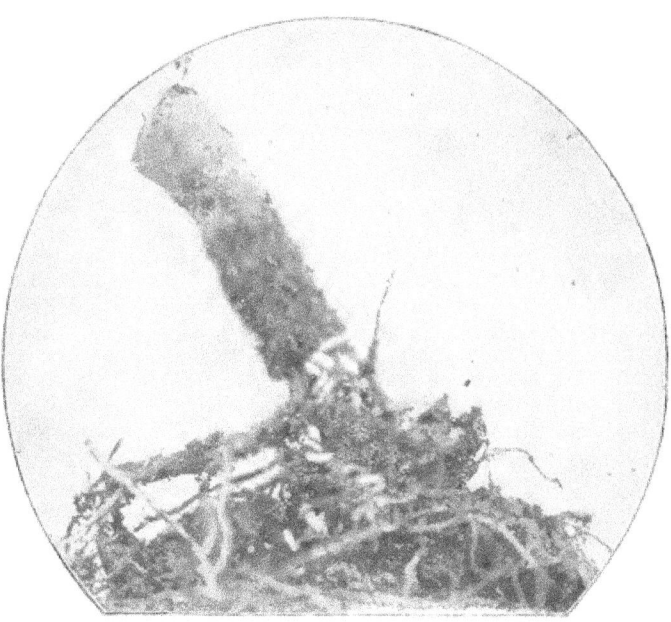

In 1886, Prof. Cook reported before the Ingham Horticultural Society that experiments at the College that year had showed conclusively that, if carefully applied and used in time, it was a specific against the maggots. Those who had reported that it would not do effective work in clay soil, or that it killed the plant, had, without doubt, deferred the application till the plants were beyond hope. A Mr. Lee, in the audience, said he had tried the liquid, and knew it would always work on clay or sand, and not hurt the plants. *He made a hole a little way from the plant.* We italicize this sentence, because it is the key-note of success with this substance. We believe that most of the reported injury to the plants has been due to the hole having been made close beside the plants so that the liquid itself reached the roots. The liquid would very quickly kill the root, but its vapor would do no harm. This point is more fully emphasized later on.

The following year, however, Prof. Cook says he is persuaded, after a through trial, that this substance cannot be made practicable. Differences in soils, and seclusion of the maggots which bore quickly out of reach of the insecticide, make its use uncertain, and therefore unsatisfactory. In 1888, Mr. Hulst reported that the substance could not be used, for when it came in contact with the roots it always did them very great injury. In 1892, in response to an inquiry from Mr. Barnhardt, the U. S. Entomologist advised him to try the liquid. Although the application was made (June 15) after many of the maggots had changed to puparia, he reported very satisfactory results.

From the above brief resume of the experiments thus far reported with this substance, we glean that the weight of evidence shows that it can usually be depended upon to kill the maggots. The only serious objections raised are that it sometimes seems not to work alike in all soils; also, it may injure the plants; and such large quantities would have to be used on radishes, onions, or turnips as to make it expensive and thus not practicable on these crops. The last objection is doubtless a valid one, unless the plants are of a choice or new variety. However, we believe, as did Prof. Cook and Mr. Lee in 1886, that when properly applied, it will prove very effective against the maggots on any soils without injuring the plants ; of course, it will work slower somewhat on the heavier soils, and the dose may have to be increased slightly on such soils.

The instrument devised by Prof. Cook in 1884, for the underground application of kerosene emulsion, apparently could not be adapted for the use of the Bisulfide of Carbon. Mr. Barnard's "Nether-inserter," devised in 1883, facilitated the making of the hole, but not the application of the liquid. Thus no instrument seemed to have been devised by which the application of the liquid could be made practicable in cabbage or cauliflower fields.

The case was stated to Mr. McGowen, the inventor of the famous McGowen Spray Nozzle. After several experiments in trying to simplify the French instrument, the idea was abandoned. He then started out on a theory of his own, and finally devised an instrument which seems to "fill the bill" quite completely. In honor of the inventor, we shall call it "The McGowen Injector." In construction, it is very simple, as the sectional drawings in fig. 17 show; the description of the different parts, and how they work are given below.

Description of the McGowen Injector.—Figure 17, B, represents a sectional view of the instrument, about one-seventh natural size. It consists of a long piston, p, its upper portion working closely in a small cylinder; the middle portion passing through the long reservoir, r; and to the lower smaller portion which passes through that part of the instrument, g, which is forced into the ground, is attached the valves, *v*, working in a cylinder attached to the lower end of the reservoir. A handle is attached to the upper end of the piston, and the lower end is pointed and works closely in the lower small cylinder only at the point opposite *g*. The reservoir is filled through the opening at *e*, which is protected by a screw cap. In B, the instrument is ready for insertion in the soil. At A, is shown a section of the lower portion of the instrument, nearly one-half natural size, and this view represents the position of the valves, *v*, when the instrument is being withdrawn from the soil. It operates very simply. When the piston is pulled up it is stopped at the proper point by the metal pin through the piston near *p*, in B. This brings the upper valve into the reservoir, *r*, and the liquid immediately fills the chamber between the two valves; this is the measuring chamber, and its size can be easily regulated to hold a teaspoonful, or more or less, by simply screwing the valves either way or by winding cloth around the piston between the valves. Before inserting in the soil, the piston is pushed down and is stopped by the lower valve striking against the bottom of its cylinder. The valves are then in the position shown in B. As the lower portion of this valve cylinder is cut out larger, the liquid escapes into this lower chamber, *l. c.*, and some runs down around the lower part of the piston but is prevented from escaping by the arrangement near the point, at *g*, by which the piston here fits very closely. The pulling up of the piston again, of course, lets the charge of liquid run out, and at the same time the measuring chamber is again filled, thus securing an automatic action. It was found necessary to have an opening in the lower chamber, *l. c.*, in order to allow air to take the place of the liquid so it could freely run into the soil. This opening, *o*, also supplies the measuring chamber with air which is drawn up into the reservoir and then displaces the liquid and allows it to freely enter the measuring chamber. All parts of the instrument are made of brass, except the small discs or leather in the valves, and the wooden handle on the piston; the reservoir may be made of tin. All parts must

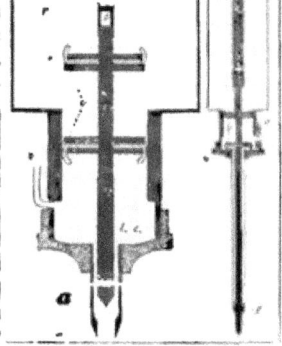

Fig. 17.—The McGowen Injector.

fit closely, ,or the liquid works through where water would not. The reservoir can be made larger or smaller, and the lower portion which is inserted in the ground can be made of any length to suit the depth to which it may sometimes be necessary to apply the liquid. On larger instruments a foot-rest could be easily attached to assist in inserting the instrument if necessary. The reservoir in our instrument (Fig. 18) is 2 feet long, 2½ inches in diameter, and holds 2 quarts of liquid.

All the parts of the injector are made of brass or tin except the simple discs of leather used in the valves, *v*. These can be easily replaced when worn. The price at which it can be made and sold will depend upon the demand and also on its size and the material of which the reservoir (*r*) is made, whether tin or brass. The reservoir in the one shown in operation in figure 18 is 2 feet long, 2½ inches in diameter, and holds about 2 quarts of the liquid. This is about the right size for use against the Cabbage Root Maggot, as one filling of the reservoir will treat about 500 plants, using a teaspoonful at each plant. It could easily be made larger without adding much weight to the instrument, for a slight increase in the diameter of the reservoir would greatly increase its capacity. Mr. McGowen can make them any size desired. The one shown in figure 18 can be made for from * $3 to $5, depending on the demand for it and the material used; in large quantities they could doubtless be made for less. The brass instrument we have has a capacity of two quarts and weighs when empty 4½ pounds, and when full of water 4 pounds more. Thus, in gardens it will require but little more than the weight of the loaded instrument to force it into the soil. But if a larger instrument was needed it might be well to have a foot-rest attached near the bottom.

A few preliminary experiments in cages here at the insectary with this substance showed that it killed, not only the maggots, but the puparia also. Scarcely a live insect could be found in the cages the next day after applying a teaspoonful of the liquid to each plant. Ten puparia were placed beneath the soil in each of two cages, and to one cage a teaspoonful of the liquid was applied and the other was left untreated. No flies ever emerged in the treated cage, while nearly every one of the puparia gave out a fly in the untreated cage. In no case did the plants show any signs of injury from the liquid. We always applied the liquid in a horizontal hole beginning about three or four inches from the plant and running down to a point a little below the roots.

But while our experiments demonstrated that the substance was sure death to the insects and did not injure the plants, we were con-

---

* Since making a quantity of them Mr. McGowan has found it neccessary to make the price $7.00 each.

vinced that to make the method practicable in the field, some method must be devised by which the liquid could be more quickly, safely and perhaps efficiently applied.

It seemed as though some instrument might be, or possibly had already been, devised by which the liquid could be thus applied. We were unable to find any record of such an instrument having been devised in this country. The "Pal-injecteur" used in France is also too extremely heavy and clumsy, and very expensive.

In fact, we believe the instrument can be so adapted as to work satisfactorily wherever the liquid is now used against underground insects. For instance, it will facilitate the application of the liquid to the new Grape Root worm (*Fidia viticida*) which has recently appeared in Ohio; and it is possible, as Prof. Cook suggested in 1880, that the Peach Borer (*Sannina exitiosa*) may be killed by the substance, especially on small trees, where it works almost entirely on the roots (we shall try some experiments in this line in the spring). Many other instances might be mentioned where it would be practicable to use the liquid, now that we have a suitable instrument to apply it. In fact, this simple and cheap injector should open up a whole field of experimentation with this liquid; why not use it against the root form of the Black Peach Aphis (discussed in Bulletin 49) or the Wooly Aphis of the apple?

The liquid is very volatile and will thus quickly evaporate if left in an open or uncorked vessel; we find large glass bottles with tight-fitting corks the best receptacles for it. The vapor is very poisonous and great care should be taken in pouring it out not to breathe much of it. As the vapor is also very explosive, no lights of any kind should be brought near when it is being used. Treat it with more care than you would gunpowder, in this respect. The best and cheapest brand now on the market is that known as "Fuma Carbon Bisulfide," manufactured by Edward R. Taylor, Cleveland, Ohio. He ships it in 10 lb. cans at 12 cents per pound, or in 50 lb. cans at 10 cents per pound. It can be obtained in small quantities at drug stores, but usually for not less than 25 cents per pound.

Thus cabbage plants can be treated once, and once is usually sufficient, at the rate of about 10 plants for 1 cent for the liquid, using about 1 teaspoonful to each plant. As the injector will last for years, and several neighbors might join in the purchase and use of one instrument, its cost would practically not influence this estimate of the cost of killing the maggots. We believe it is the cheapest, most effective, and most practicable method yet devised for fighting this pest on crops of cabbages and cauliflowers; on crops of radishes, turnips, or onions, it will probably be too expensive, except where choice or new varieties are attacked. The Carbolic Acid Emulsion will prove the most practicable on these last crops.

The method of inserting the injector is shown in figure 18. The hole should always begin at a distance of 3 or 4 inches from the plant and run horizontally downward to a point a little below the roots. To accomplish this, the injector must be inserted at an angle, as shown in the figure. Force it down until you think the point is a little below the roots, then let out the charge of liquid. In operating the injector, first pull the piston up as far as it will go; this loads the measuring chamber between the valves; then push down the piston until it stops, and the instrument is ready to be pushed into the ground. Push it into the ground as far as desired, hold it there while you pull up the piston; by this operation you let the charge out of the lower chamber into the ground, and at the same time the measuring chamber is again filled. Hold the injector in the ground

FIG. 18.—The McGowen Injector, and how to use it.

a few seconds after the piston has been pulled up in order that all the liquid in the charge may have a chance to run out. Then pull the injector out of the ground, and quickly, with the foot, fill the hole with earth and step on it to pack it down. Press down the piston, and you are ready to treat the next plant. Never push the injector in the ground unless the piston is clear down, because if the lower end is not thus closed it will immediately fill with soil, which is not easily removed. Study the drawings in figure 17 in connection with these directions and you will understand the reason for each step. We would advise that the reservoir be first filled with water and the injector operated above the ground until each step is thoroughly understood. There is nothing complicated about the instrument, or the way it is to be operated. It can be easily taken apart and cleaned if necessary; the only caution to be observed in replacing the parts is to have the flanges of the leather in the upper valve turned upward.

We recently tested the effect of the liquid on some young cabbage plants not yet large enough to set in the field. A tablespoonful of the liquid was applied beneath several plants with the injector. In a few minutes the odor of the liquid was very noticeable on the surface around the plants. These plants have not shown any signs of injury from this large dose. As stated in the description of figure 17, the amount of liquid to be applied can be easily regulated. On small plants, a teaspoonful will probably be sufficient. When the plants are well established in the field, and the maggots thick, use a tablespoonful. One application will usually suffice. The time to apply will be when the maggots are first discovered, early in May. Do not wait until the plants begin to wilt before making the application, for although it will then kill the insects, it will not reinvigorate the plant.

We believe gardeners will find this the most practicable and most effective method of killing the Cabbage Root Maggot when it attacks cabbages and cauliflowers.--[*From Bulletin 78, p. 531, November, 1894.*]

REMEDY FOR PHYLLOXERA.

The introduction of American plants to replace those destroyed by parasites in French vineyards has not arrested the use of insecticides for the protection of French vines still attacked by *Phylloxera*, and for this purpose Carbon Bisulphide (either pure or dissolved in water), sulpho-carbonates and submersion continue to be employed with more or less success. The Carbon Bisulphide is by far the more efficient, but is too volatile and does not diffuse with sufficient rapidity. When, however, it is mixed with vaseline, its volatility is reduced and its diffusibility is increased, the former proving advantageous in light and calcareous soils, the latter in heavy soils, in accordance with theoretical considerations. The vaselined sulphide is applied in the same way as the ordinary sulphide, depositing some at the foot of the vine stock and spreading the rest over the surface; this treatment is found to be effectual; with it *Phylloxera* is no longer seen in the roots, vegetation is luxuriant, and numerous new rootlets indicate a decisive increase in vitality ; the manuring on a test tract of land had not been altered for six years, therefore the improvement was solely due to the insecticide.—*P. Cazeneuve.*

REMEDIES FOR SUBTERRANEAN INSECTS.

U. S. Department of Agriculture. Farmers Bulletin No. 19.

BISULFIDE OF CARBON.—This is the great French remedy for the phylloxera, 150,000 acres being now subjected to treatment with it, and applies equally well to all other root-inhabiting lice. The treatment is made at any season except the period of ripening of the fruit, and consists in making holes about the vines 1 foot to 16 inches deep and pouring into each about one-half ounce of Bisulfide and closing the hole with the foot. These injections are made about 1½ feet apart, and not closer to the vines than 1 foot. It is better to make a large number of small doses than a few large ones. Hand injectors and injecting plows are employed in France to put the Bisulfide into the soil about the vines, but a short stick or iron bar may be made to take the place of these injectors for limited tracts.

For root maggots a teaspoonful is poured into a hole at the base of the plant, covering as above.

For fuller information on the Grape-root worm, readers are referred to the valuable articles in the Ohio Farmer, from Prof. F. M. Webster, Entomologist of the Agricultural Experimental Station at Wooster, O. Oct. 25, 1894, page 337. Nov. 1, 1894, page 357. Dec. 6, 1894, page 453. Dec. 27, 1894 page 505.

EFFECT OF CARBON BISULPHID ON THE YIELD OF CROPS.

A. GIRARD.

[From Vol. VI, No. 6, Experiment Station Record.]

In view of the increasing use of bisulfide of carbon for the destruction of subterranean insects, as root lice, root maggots, white grubs, ants in their nests, etc., a knowledge of the effects of this substance on soils and vegetation becomes important. That it will destroy plant life when used excessively is abundantly proven with the phylloxera of the grape of Europe. In the first experiment with this substance vines were frequently killed by overdosing, and the treatment d'extinction, as employed in Switzerland and some other European countries outside of France, consists of using it in such quantities that the infested vines and lice are destroyed at the same time. L. O. Howard states that in an experience of his in destroying an ant nest the grass immediately surrounding was killed. With these facts in mind it is interesting to note that this substance seems to have a strikingly beneficial effect on the soil in greatly increasing its fertility. This seems to be conclusively shown in an elaborate series of experiments conducted by the author and extending over a number of years. Attention was first called to this action by the results following an attempt to destroy a nematode (Heterodera schachtii) upon the roots of the sugar beet. To kill the parasite, protected as it was in the substance of the beet, it was necessary to use the bisulfide at the rate of 9½ oz. to the square yard, or 2,904 lbs. to the acre, which resulted in the complete sacrifice of the beet crop. Wheat grown on the same field the year following, however, exhibited a remarkable superiority throughout the tract treated with the insecticide, and this led in the following years to a series of trials at the same rate.

The results the second year after the original treatment, without further additions of the bisulfide or use of fertilizers, were as marked as in the first year's crops. The explanation of this increased vigor of plant growth is not altogether satisfactory. It is supposed that the bisulfide acts as a stimulant to vegetation and also poisons subterranean insects or other organisms, crypto gamic, perhaps, which otherwise would injuriously affect the roots of plants. It may also exert some chemical action on the soil elements, resulting in their easier assimilation by plants.

These results, with accompanying explanations, are in contrast with, but not necessarily contradictory to, the commonly held idea that the use of bisulfide of carbon is liable to stop the nitrification or conversion into plant food of the vegetable matters in the soil by destroying the microscopic germs which bring this about. But this experiment indicates, at least, that benefit rather than injury to the soil in its productive capacity is to be anticipated where the substance is employed in the ordinary application in vineyards, or at about one-tenth the rate given above, viz.: a little less than 1 oz. to the square yard, or 290 lbs. to the acre, with a minimum rate of 175 lbs. to the acre.

FURTHER CONTRIBUTIONS ON CARBON BISULPHIDE TREATMENT OF SOILS.

B. Heinze. Centr. Bakt. Parasitenk., Zweite Abth., 18 [1|3], 56-74; [7|9], 246-64; [13|15], 462-70; [24|25], 790-8 (1907).—Soil treated with CS_2 gave a better yield of potatoes, rye, oats, sugar-beets and grapes than did untreated soil. The CS_2 works directly on the micro-organisms of the soil retarding the growth of some, stimulating the growth of others, and besides, it acts indirectly on the mineral constituents of the soil. CS_2 increases the available nutriment by giving a more active growth of micro-organisms, moulds, bacteria, etc., which produce CO_2 and organic acids, and by forming some H_2SO_3 through the oxidation of S. These acids then dissolve some of the mineral salts in the soil. Ca, K, and Mg were found to be increased, but the author could not prove that the available phosphates were increased. CS_2 works differently on the different organisms, such as algae, moulds, yeasts and bacteria. The micro-organism which brings about fermentation was restrained and the N assimilating micro-organisms especially azotobacter, were favored by the consequent preservation of a rich supply of carbon in the form of pectin, soluble humus material, pentosan, etc. In brief, CS_2 produces a satisfactory soil condition for the N collecting micro-organisms especially azotobacter. CS_2 inhibits the growth of plant parasites of an animal nature. How it affects parasites of a plant nature, is yet to be determined. By the CS_2 treatment, however, soil can be easily freed from weeds. CS_2 treated soil retains its moisture better than untreated soil and in sandy soils, nitrification is lessened, and the loss of nitrate by leaching is reduced. By the addition of a small amount of CS_2 to the soil shortly before cultivation, it is possible to determine which plants secure their N, mainly from nitrate, and which from ammonia, since the CS_2 inhibits nitrification for a time, so that the plants must obtain their N from ammonia directly. CS_2 is of great value in overcoming soil sickness (Bodenmüdigkeitsercheinungen) in case of vines, peas and clover. Oberlin has shown that the soil sickness of vineyards, which in many regions occurs periodically, can be counteracted by treating the soil with CS_2. Clover sickness was remedied by treating the soil with CS_2 and the nodules developed despite the treatment. The author would explain the improvement in these cases by the inhibition of the micro-organisms which produce the toxic condition, since, in distinction from soil exhaustion, soil sickness is not remedied by fertilizers. Sterilization improved vine development in these soils but not in normal soil. Before replanting vineyards it is necessary to allow the soil to rest for some time. This resting time is shortened by the use of CS_2 and further, such treatment gives a better growth to the vine and a better ripening of the grapes. Thiocarbonates, sulphates, mustard oils and even green mustard will work on the soil as CS_2 does.

M. X. Sullivan.

DEATH TO INSECTS.

Have no more Insects in your Mill. Fuma Carbon Bisulfide does the Work.

Please read the following letters from those who have used it, also Bulletin 58, Agricultural College of Michigan.

Messrs. A. WILHELM & SONS, Defiance, Ohio, write:

E. R. TAYLOR,

Dear Sir:—Your last dose of three 50-pound cans of your Bisulfide settled the weevil family in our mill, and we had our mill so full that we were about giving possession. Thanks to your Bisulfide. We have referred our neighbors to you for relief. Mill 60x70, four stories.   A. WILHELM & SONS.

EXTERMINATING GRAIN WEEVIL.

Editor American Elevator and Grain Trade:—I notice in the June number of the AMERICAN ELEVATOR AND GRAIN TRADE that "Sangamon" asks in No. 65 of "Queries and Replies" for information regarding the use of Carbon Bisulfide as a means of exterminating insects in grain. Having had practical experience in this matter, I think I can give him some points about it that may be of use to him.

In the first place he asks how much should be used. For a wheat bin full of grain use 1½ pounds per ton of grain in order to make certain. When the bin is empty use about one pound to 1,000 cubic feet of space. For instance, in the case of a bin 20x20x20 feet as given by "Sangamon," about eight pounds would be needed. A small room 10 feet each way would by the same rule require one pound.

As to the cost at wholesale, I would say it can be purchased in 50 pound cans for 15 cents per pound. However, a much cheaper rate can be had from the manufacturer. Edward R. Taylor, a chemist of Cleveland, O., sent me on my order 100 pounds for $10.00.

This Carbon Bisulfide will kill all kinds of insects, bugs and beetles, and when thoroughly applied will destroy every one of them in the building, no matter where hidden. It is not so injurious to human life as some other vapors, but it is explosive when mixed with air, and therefore great care should be taken not to bring any kind of a light near while it is being applied. It evaporates so quickly that it can be thrown on any grain without injuring it in any way.

The vapor of Carbon Bisulfide is heavier than that of air, and it naturally follows that when the liquid is thrown on grain, its vapor will sink down through the space between the kernels and so penetrate the whole bin. The bin or room must be very tight, the more nearly air-tight the better, otherwise the vapor will escape and be lost. After opening the can in which the Bisulfide is received, no time should be wasted, but the contents should be at once scattered in the bins and the doors or covers closed as quickly as possible, and kept closed about twenty-four hours, to give time for the vapor to act and reach every corner.

The above is the method I followed with satisfactory results, and I have since had no trouble with insects of any kind. By keeping every part of the building clean, well ventilated and well lighted, the insects can be kept down, as they do not thrive in clean houses.

Respectfully, T. C.

I do not know who wrote this letter T. C.

WEEVIL IN WHEAT.

This last year has developed a new trouble for the millers and farmers to contend with, viz.: weevil. They have appeared where they were never seen before, and before the farmer was aware of it his wheat was practically ruined by this pest. A reporter for the *Herald-Despatch* called on the Shellabarger Mill and Elevator Company to ascertain whether or not the millers had any trouble in this respect and learned from the secretary of the company, W. L. Shellabarger, that they were using a preparation called Bisulfide of Carbon. With this they have practically exterminated the weevil in their elevators, but are compelled to use it occasionally, owing to the fact that fresh deliveries of wheat bring in more weevil. They have used this chemical for several years with most satisfactory results and would recommend it to anyone who has to contend with weevil.—*Decatur, Ill.*

WEDDLE & SUTTON,
  Merchant Millers,

WEST NEWTON, PA., July 3, '94.

Mr. E. R. Taylor.

Dear Sir:—The Bisulfide you sent us is all you claimed for it. We used about 100 lbs. on about 7,000 bushels of wheat infested with Black Weevil and have not seen a live one in the wheat since.

Have sold some we had left to a farmer to use in his granaries to kill weevil. We propose to keep it for sale.

Ship us by freight 100 lbs. more, and oblige.

Yours truly,
WEDDLE & SUTTON.

ENTOMOLOGY.

PANTRY, STORE-HOUSE, AND MILL PESTS.
[By Gerald McCarthy, Entomologist, N. C. Experiment Station.]

ONE of the most dangerous insects which infest flour mills in some parts of the country is the so called Mediterranean Flour Moth (*Ephestia Kuhniella*.) This insect is known to exist in North Carolina, and probably exists in Tennessee. It is likely to become a most serious and expensive pest. Figure 1 shows the appearance of this insect in different stages of growth.

This insect is of obscure nativity, but is thought to be American by European entomologists. It first became troublesome on this continent in Canada in 1889. In the province of Ontario it infested several large flouring and patent food mills to such an extent as to compel the stoppage of the works for several weeks while all the hands were put to work cleaning and fumigating the mills. The loss to several of these establishments, including stock and bolting cloths ruined, and loss of time and labor, must have exceeded $1,000 each.

The moth which produces this destructive caterpillar is a slender lead-colored insect, about one inch long. The wings have wavy black lines near the tip. The insect is rather sluggish and often remains in one position for

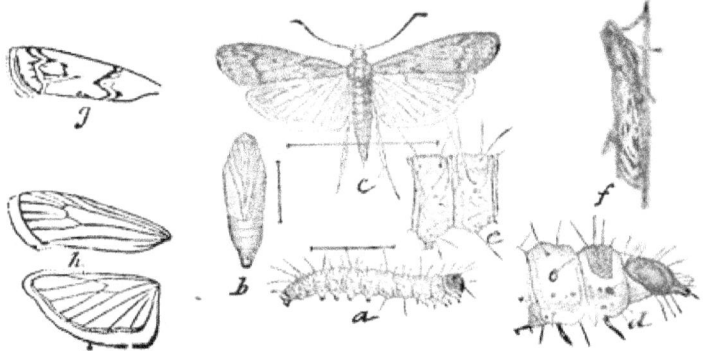

FIG. 1.—MEDITERRANEAN FLOUR MOTH.
a, caterpillar; *b*, pupa; *c*, adult; *d*, head and fore-part of caterpillar; *e*, hind-part of caterpillar; *f*, adult moth seen from side; *h*, *i*, views of wings. The hair lines show exact size.

a long time. This moth can probably be found active in this state in all the months of the year except January. The eggs are whitish or pink, and kidney-shaped. The eggs are usually laid on outside of sacks and in the cracks of bins. They hatch in about twenty days. As soon as hatched the caterpillar makes its way into the flour and there spins around itself a silken tunnel in which it lives and feeds on the flour. These tunnels cause the flour to become knotted into clots which refuse to pass through the machinery, rendering the material worthless.

Remedy.—The only practicable remedy for this pest is to fumigate the entire mill and building in which flour and manufactured foods are kept, with Carbon Bisulfide.

This substance is a fluid having a most disgusting odor. It vaporizes readily when exposed to the air and in this condition is destructive to all forms of active insect life. To use it, the room or building to be fumigated must be closed as tightly as possible. All interior doors should be kept open. Expose the liquid in shallow pans or saucers and close the building for twenty-four to forty-eight hours. Then open all doors and windows and allow the gas to disperse in the air. Care should be exercised to avoid breathing the gas and on no account should any fire or light be brought into the room or building while the peculiar odor can be smelled. This substance is highly explosive and inflammable. With care no harm will follow its use. When

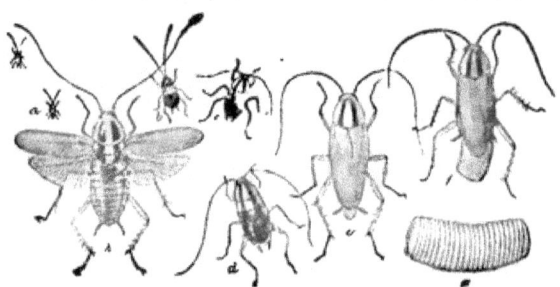

FIG. 2.—GERMAN COCKROACH OR CROTON BUG.

a, Roach just hatched; *b*, a little older; *c*, half grown; *d*, nearly full grown; *e*, adult; *f*, female with egg case; *g*, egg case enlarged; *h*, adult with wings spread.

the gas disperses in the air it leaves no residue behind, so that no trace of it can be found in the flour or food. Where only a small lot of goods or sacks are infested they may be placed in an air-tight room or bin, and a dish of the liquid placed within near the top. Use about four fluid ounces of the liquid for each twenty-five cubic feet of space, or for grain or flour in a tight bin use one pound of Carbon Bisulfide for each ton. Carbon Bisulfide can be bought of W. S. Powell & Co., Baltimore, Md., and of Edward Clark, Columbus, O. Price about 20 cents per pound in 5 pound cans. In smaller quantities it can be had of any druggist.

THE COCKROACH—*Periplaneta orientalis*, and other species.—The cockroach is one of the most common, disgusting and troublesome pests in all places where flour or bread is kept. There are two species about equally common in the Southern States. The larger one is dark-brown and varies from three-fourths to one inch in length. It runs very rapidly, and being so flat, it easily finds shelter in some crack when pursued. Figure 2 represents the common yellow roach, or "croton bug." It is much smaller than the other species.

All roaches are enormously fecund, all are voracious, and eat every kind of food used by people. They prefer bread and flour and foods made of flour. These pests are nocturnal in their habits, and hence are apt to escape observation until their numbers increase so much as to render their presence alarmingly patent.

Remedy.—Cleanliness where such is practical is essential to keep free of these insects. In mills and warehouses where flour dust and grain is everywhere, the Carbon Bisulfide fumigation must be resorted to, and must be very thoroughly done, so that the vapor of the substance will find its way into the cracks and crevices where these pests hide. In addition, pyrethrum powder should be blown into the cracks where they are known to hide, or pure kerosene oil may be blown in with an ordinary oiling can. Powdered borax sprinkled on shelves where they run will drive them away. Old rags moistened with molasses water in which Paris green has been suspended will poison them. The cloths should be freshly moistened each evening and removed in the morning.

THE GRAIN AND RICE WEEVIL *(Calandra)*—Two Species.—In the Southern States we have two species of grain weevil, *Calandra granarius*, which infests wheat and corn, and *Calandra oryzæ*, which infests rice in warehouses. The first is the more common and injurious. Both species are much alike.

Fig 3 shows a back and side view of a weevil of this family, but this is much larger than the true grain or rice weevil. The grain weevil is dark-brown, or nearly black, is very slender and about one-eighth of an inch long.

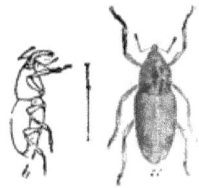

FIG 3.—GRAIN WEEVIL.

Immense quantities of wheat corn and rice are annually destroyed by these pests in warehouses, stores and homes. The only practicable remedy for these pests is Carbon Bisulfide The infected grain should be put in an air tight box or bin and a dish of the liquid laid on top of the heap. The whole must then be tightly covered and left for twenty-four to forty-eight hours. Then expose to the air until all odor is gone. The grain or flour will not be injured by the carbon. Use at the rate of one and a half to two pounds for each ton of grain, and cover tightly so as to keep in the fumes until the insects are killed. They are exceedingly tenacious of life.

THE FLAT FLOUR BEETLE.-*Silvanus Surinaminsis.*-This is a narrow brown beetle one-twelfth inch long, and scarcely thicker than a sheet of paper. It is a native of Asia, as its name betokens. It is becoming yearly a greater pest in the Southern States, and will probably exceed in mischief even the Calandra weevils. The remedy for this is the same as for the others—Carbon Bisulfide. This insect is fond of greasy substances, and if some paper is soaked in melted lard and Paris green sprinkled upon it while moist, and the poisoned sheets distributed on floors and shelves whre grain and flour is kept, many of the beetles will be killed; but this plan will not give satisfaction where they are already abundant, being too slow in its operation. The carbon will kill most of them in a very short time when it is properly used.

As a matter of safety all mills, warehouses and stores where grain, flour and food-stuffs are kept, should receive a thorough annual cleaning, and fumigation with Carbon Bisulfide. This, if attended to and thoroughly done, will save many thousands of dollars' damage. It will be most efficacious if done about April 1. It may be repeated with benefit in July or August.

Web of the Mediterranean Flour Moth.

FIGHTING THE MOTH.
By L. C. S.

My experience with the Mediterranean flour moth is of nearly seven years' standing. Until I took charge of this mill six years ago I had never seen or heard of the insect, and when I found it here and learned what it was I doubted whether such a delicate little creature could do any more harm than a housefly. I soon had evidence, however, of its capacity for mischief. For one day it actually succeeded in shutting down our 100 h. p. engine by so choking conveyors, elevators, etc., with its webs that the wheels simply could not turn. This is an absolute fact.

Meanwhile I had written to Prof. Johnson, the entomologist, about the pest and sent him a sample of its work, so when the mill was finally choked to a standstill I knew what to do. I first put six men at work taking spouts and elevator legs apart and cleaning them thoroughly, and when that was done I had them go for the machines. It took us just six days to get cleaned up. Under the Professor's advice I had provided ten gallons of bisulphide of carbon and about 200 tin pie-plates, and when Saturday afternoon came we closed and packed all the doors and windows, distributed the plates throughout the mill, filled them with bisulphide, and "let her simmer" until Monday morning, when on opening up the mill we found dead moths everywhere. The destruction was so thorough that for three months or more things ran along without trouble. Then the spouts and conveyors began to fill up with webs again, until at the end of six months we were compelled to clean up and repeat the dose. In fact we did not get wholly rid of the moth until about two years ago, when, on changing our mill over to the sifter system, we took out all elevator belts, took the legs apart and scraped them, took down all the wooden spouts, burned them up, and put in their places adjustable galvanized iron spouts. That was the end of our trouble from moths, and I believe that so long as we keep our mill clean and the main floors well whitewashed they will let us severely alone.—The Roller Mill, November, 1900.

Bulletin No. 9, of the Experiment Station of Florida, states: "Bins and corn cribs can be easily rid of ants, weevil, rats, mice, beetles, etc., if the room be made air tight, and occasionally filled from the top with the vapor of Bisulfide of Carbon. This is the only way in which our farmers ever will keep corn, peas, etc., from insect attacks. In this way a terrible waste will be checked, and the thousands of dollars now spent for "shipped corn" be saved the state.

BISULFIDE OF CARBON.

From the Appendix to the Nineteenth Report of the State Entomologist of Illinois. By W. G. Johnson, A. M., Assistant Entomologist.

The simplest, most effective, and least expensive remedy for all mill pests is bisulfide of carbon, a very inflammable, volatile, foul-smelling liquid, as clear as water. Its vapor is heavier than air and will penetrate every crack and crevice in a mill or warehouse when used in sufficient quantities. It can be thrown directly upon grain without injuring its edible qualities, and will not affect its vitality in the least. In mills it can be used about the machinery, spouts and elevators with perfect assurance that the manufactured products will not be damaged. It is a powerful insecticide, the atmosphere produced by its vapors being sure death to insects, as well as to rats and mice. I know of no instance, however, where the slightest deleterious effect has been realized by persons applying it in mills, although they unavoidably inhale some of the fumes.

The amount of liquid to be used depends (1) on the size of the building, (2) on its tightness, and (3) on the magnitude of the attack. Where the building is reasonably tight and but slightly infested, one pound of bisulfide is sufficient for every thousand cubic feet of air space. If it is somewhat open or badly infested the amount should be doubled. When applied to bins containing stored grain, one pound of the liquid to every hundred bushels of grain is commonly used; but if the insects are very abundant the amount of bisulphide should be doubled.

A number of methods for application of bisulfide of carbon have been suggested and tested, but the most effective manner of applying it in mills consists in simply pouring the liquid into shallow dishes, such as soup plates, or pans, and distributing them about the building. Bits of cotton-waste saturated with the liquid should also be thrust into spouts, elevator legs, machines and other places where the pests usually congregate in great numbers. Spraying or throwing the liquid broadcast into badly infested corners, on machines, and other pieces of apparatus where the pests are particularly abundant, has been attended with very good results.

Saturday afternoon is the best time for fumigating a mill. After sweeping it from top to bottom, using a "steam sweeper" where it is practicable, all fires about the premises should be extinguished and the mill closed as tightly as possible. The dishes and cotton-waste should be previously distributed, so that there will be no unnecessary delay in the application of the foul-smelling fluid. The distribution of these vessels must of course depend, as already stated, upon the condition of the mill and the severity of the attack. It is best to begin with the lowest story and work up, as the operators can then keep above the settling gas. When the bisulphide has been applied throughout the mill it should be locked and kept closed until the following Monday morning. All windows and doors should then be thrown wide open and the building allowed to air an hour before any fire is started. Where the building is large and a great quantity of bisulphide has been used, it would be wise to observe the extra precaution of stationing a watchman without to prevent any one from entering the building during fumigation.

As a guide to millers who may use this method for exterminating insect pests in mills, I will quote several letters from practical millers who have used bisulphide of carbon successfully. The superintendent of a large Pennsylvania milling company, whose name is withheld by request, under date of July 12, 1895, wrote me the following letter, which is a valuable contribution to this subject, and should be read by every wide-awake miller and grain dealer:

"We have delayed answering your valued favor of May last until we were able to report the result of our efforts to destroy the weevils in our mill. Following in the line of your advice, we ran our stock down and thoroughly renovated our mill from top to bottom, cleaning all reels and purifiers. We then fumigated the whole mill with bisulphide of carbon. We distributed 300 soup plates about half filled with bisulfide through the mill, and saturated balls of cotton with the same material and placed them in all the reels and purifiers. This we did on Saturday night, and closed the mill tight and left the weevils to their destruction.

"We opened the mill Monday morning and thoroughly ventilated it before starting. We found that we had destroyed thousands, and in the reels and purifiers we had killed them all. In the course of a few days, however they began to show up in the cracks in the floors all over the mill, and in dark corners. Two weeks later we repeated the dose of bisulfide in the same manner and obtained about the same results. In the meantime, however, we whitewashed the mill from top to bottom; that is, every place that could be covered, putting on a good heavy coat. We have not destroyed them all by any means; but we have reduced their forces to a very small number. Eternal vigilance is the order of the day.

"We are still fighting them. Our plan is to keep a stock of bisulfide on hand outside of the main building, as we do not think it advisable to store it in the mill on account of its inflammable nature. Wherever we find a place infested by the weevil we use it freely, taking care to do it when the mill is shut down and closed up tight. We find the best results from the use of bisulfide of carbon can be obtained by spraying it on the floors and infested places. We think when placed in plates it does not evaporate quick enough to produce the death atmosphere required. Before closing let us return our sincere thanks to you for the interest you have taken in the matter, and assure you that we appreciate your valuable advice."

The "American Miller," for July, 1905, contains another interesting and valuable communication on this subject, from Mr. H. J. Laurie, of Norwalk, Ohio, and I quote it here in full:

"As the season is now upon us when a large majority of the iron spouts. That was the end of our trouble for months, and I flouring mills of the country are being troubled with insects of various kinds, such as weevils, worms, moths, etc., I thought it might not be out of place to give our experience here with bisulfide of carbon, which we have been using for several seasons with very satisfactory results.

"I have reason to believe that a number of millers have used this remedy with very indifferent results, owing, in my opinion, to the manner in which it was applied. In the first place, the mill should be thoroughly swept (as every mill should be daily), and if there are any broken panes of glass in the windows they should be replaced, the object being to make the mill tight as possible. Then have a number of shallow tin pans, say, about fifty to every 100 pounds of the compound used. Begin at the bottom of the mill, and place the pans where the insects are the thickest. It is best for two to go together, one placing the pans, the other filling them, using a watering can or something of the kind having a spout.

"I apply it to the bolting reel and flour garners as follows: I get ready, beforehand, a number of medium sized bunches of cotton-waste, two for each reel, with a string attached to each. I dip these bunches into the bucket of compound, pressing out with a paddle so they will not drip too much; then throw them under the reel and down the conveyor, leaving the string on the outside so they can be recovered, then close the doors of the bolting chest tightly. I suspend one or two bunches in like manner in the flour garners and screening bins. In applying it to the wheat bins we level off the grain and place the pans on it filled with the liquid. By applying it in this way to wheat bins and taking proper care to have the bins emptied and swept out occasionally, no one need be troubled with weevils in their grain elevators. There is one thing that we have discovered, and that is that the compound must be reasonably fresh when used. If kept for any great length of time it loses its strength, consequently it should be used as soon as practicable after receiving it, and no more should be ordered than it is intended to use.

"Before commencing the use of bisulfide of carbon this mill was badly infested with weevils and other insects. Now we are nearly free from the pests. I do not say that this remedy will kill every insect in a mill. I do not think there is an insectcide made powerful enough to reach every nook and crevice, such as we have in mills; but we do know that by a judicious use of bisulfide of carbon in warm weather, when the insects are in full force, and by a due regard to cleanliness all over the mill, any mill can be rid of the pests.

"The compound being highly inflammable, there should be no fire or lights used in the mill at the time it is applied. The best time to apply it is Saturday evening, and the mill should be kept closed till Monday morning."

There have been so many exaggerated reports about the nature of this chemical compound that it is necessary to give a few notes regarding it in this place. In this connection I can do no greater service than to quote a letter from Mr. Edward R. Taylor, of Penn Yan, N. Y., the leading manufacturer of bisulfide of carbon in this country. It appeared in the "American Miller" for Sepember, 1895, and read as follows:

"Editor 'American Miller:' I have seen a great many very random statements on the subject of the inflammability of bisulfide of carbon. One says, 'Use the same care as with gunpowder.' Another says, 'It is a very explosive liquid.' These are both very misleading statements with reference to the properties of bisulfide of carbon. I have quoted the statements, however, in my printed matter for the reason that farmers and many others use the goods, and will be sufficiently startled by such statements to be careful and have no light or fire about.

"Nearly everybody is now familiar with gasoline. The properties of that liquid and bisulfide are practically identical in that both are inflammable but neither of them explosive. The vapor of either of them mixed with air is explosive, but the liquids are not explosive. I have shipped thousands of pounds of bisulfide to millers, elevator operators, and farmers in the last few years, and I have yet to have the first report of any disaster, even of the most trivial character, from a single one of them. Need I say more? My directions, are explicit. Do the work Saturday afternoon by daylight. Absolutely have no light or fire of any kind about. Close the mill and leave the bugs to their destruction till Monday morning. Then open doors and windows, and thoroughly ventilate before going to work."

Some of the insurance companies have commenced to feel a little uneasy lest they should suffer loss by fire originating from the use of bisulfide of carbon in mills. The "American Miller" has investigated this subject by sending letters of inquiry to all the more important millers' insurance companies in the United States and Canada, and so far has not learned of a single fire which is known to have been caused by the use of bisulfide of carbon. The properties of the fluid have been fully described repeatedly, and millers have been warned to keep lights and fire away from the vapor, lest an explosion should occur. The fact that it has been used so long without fires being traceable to it, gives strength to the opinion that millers, out of consideration for their own lives, have heeded the warning and have been exceedingly careful in applying it. When they become more familiar with its use they may grow careless, but we hope such will not be the case. It should not be stored near the mill as this increases the fire risk. A break in the can might unexpectedly release fumes which would soon fill the mill.

Bisulfide of carbon is sold at drug stores at from 20 to 30 cents a pound, but can be bought much cheaper at wholesale, directly from the manufacturer. A grade known as "Fuma Bisulfide of Carbon" can be obtained directly from its manufacturer, Mr. Edward R. Taylor, Penn Yan, N. Y., in fifty or hundred-pound cans at ten cents a pound, and is much more effective than the ordinary grades on the market. A carefully prepared circular containing full information for its use and the necessary precautions to be heeded during its application is sent with each order sold.

Flemingsburg, Ky., Oct. 7, 1898.
Mr. Edward R. Taylor, Cleveland, Ohio.

Dear Sir: Please send us as soon as possible two fifty-pound cans of your Bisulfide to destroy bugs and worms in wheat. We tried it last winter and found it very effective in ridding our wheat of bugs and worms. Very truly,

W. S. FANT.

Harrisville, West Va., Oct. 6, 1898.
Mr. Edward R. Taylor, Cleveland, O.

Dear Sir: We received your fifty-pound can of Carbon Bisulfide and have used enough of it to know it will do the work. You will find enclosed money order for which please send us 50 pounds more via Pennsboro, and oblige.
Yours truly, HARRISVILLE MILL CO.

Manti, Utah, August 1, 1899.
Edward R. Taylor, Manufacturing Chemist.

Dear Sir: Please ship me 100 pounds of your Fuma Bisulfide of Carbon; Will remit upon receipt of invoice. Had 50 pounds of your medicine several years ago and it is good stuff.
Yours truly, L. F. BECKER.

Edward R. Taylor, Cleveland, O.

Dear Sir: Enclosed please find check for $20.00 in full payment of invoice of May 31st. We are delighted with the results obtained from your Fuma. Respectfully yours,

D. E. FAUL MILLING CO.

ADDRESS

AT THE

Farmers' Institute, Manassas, Va.
February 22, 1893

ON

THE "FLY WEEVIL."

(*Gelechia cerealella*)

By L. O. Howard, Assistant Entomologist, U. S. Department Agriculture, Washington, D. C.

The State of Virginia seems to be the original American home of this destructive grain pest. Originally, without a doubt, a European insect, it was unquestionably imported by the early settlers of Virginia in their supplies of wheat brought from the old country. From this center it has spread in all directions through the country, but more extensively and injuriously towards the South than towards the North, since it does not thrive in a very cold climate. South of the wheat belt it is a very serious enemy to corn, reaching its maximum as a corn pest in Texas. In the extreme Northern States it is frequently found in grain which is stored, for one purpose or another, in buildings which are artificially warmed, but although frequently carried North during the summer in grain, it dies out in course of time in cold storehouses or mills. It affects not only corn and wheat, but all other stored cereal products.

The best of the early writings upon this subject are by Virginians. At the beginning of the present century it was investigated by Mr. Landon Carter, and later Mr. Edmund Ruffin, a well-known writer upon agricultural topics, and the man who first suggested the value of marl as a fertilizer, paid some attention to this pest, and wrote several very able articles upon its habits and the best measures to be taken against it. Since the war of the literature upon this insect has been devoted to a consideration of its habits as a corn pest in the South, and only recently have its injuries to the wheat crop of Virginia and Maryland become so serious as to attract general attention. Professor Riley published a general article upon the species in his report as entomologist of the Department of Agriculture for 1884, and within the last year Prof. E. W. Doran, late entomologist of the Maryland Agricultural Experiment Station, published a good account of the insect upon pages 437-441 of Bulletin XVI. of the Station.

The farmers of Virginia are particularly concerned with the damage done by this insect to the wheat crop. Its habits need not to be dilated upon, since they are doubtless familiar to all concerned in its treatment. It may be stated briefly, however, that the parent insect is a small gray moth or "candle fly" resembling a clothes' moth. This moth lays its eggs only upon hard grain. The eggs hatch into small, whitish, maggot-like caterpillars, which eat out the interior of the individual grains, and when full grown spin delicate silk cocoons, from which the moths eventually issue. The insect passes the winter only in your barns and store-houses. It will breed uninterruptedly, generation after generation, in stored wheat. After the time of harvest the moth flies out from the granaries to the wheat fields, and will lay its eggs upon grains of wheat in the shocks. The larvae are not destroyed in the threshing, and are carried back to the granaries again. From these facts it is plain that if the granaries of a neighborhood are kept free from the insect the shocks will not become infested in the fields. If an individual farmer, however, takes the trouble to disinfect his granary, his wheat shocks will be infested by moths flying from the barns of his neighbors, provided he does not thresh very soon after harvest, or before the eggs hatch and the larvae penetrate the individual grains. In such cases early threshing is very important. I realize the difficulty which frequently occurs in getting the thresher at the proper time, and where the wheat must be left in the field, the individual farmer must disinfect his granary every year soon after the wheat is put in. There is an alternative, however, and it is a most desirable alternative, and upon its practice depends the diminution of the insect in numbers, if not its practical extermination, in any given neighborhood. Let all of the wheat growers of a neighborhood, by concerted action, disinfect their granaries thoroughly for one or two years. It is plain that if this be done all future damage will depend upon the importation of the insect in cereal products from some other locality. This is a plan which is eminently fitting that a body of farmers like this should take into earnest consideration, provided the amount of damage annually done by this pest would seem to warrant the trouble and expense.

How is the disinfecting to be done? A malodorous, inflammable liquid known as bisulfide of carbon, is the agent, and its application is very simple. The simplicity of the operation depends upon the fact that the liquid is extremely volatile. When exposed to the air it evaporates with great rapidity, and its vapor is sure death to insect life. Professor Doran, in the Bulletin of the Maryland Agricultural Experiment Station, above referred to, following earlier writers, recommends the use of this substance in tight bins, and when so used it is, undoubtedly, more effective; but there is no absolute necessity for a very tight receptacle, and it may be used to advantage in a reasonably close room of any dimensions. The method is to pour the liquid into shallow vessels, like small tin pans, and set them on top of the grain. The vapor is heavier than air, and will sink down through the mass of grain and destroy all insects. The amount to be used varies with the space to be treated. When used in bins, a pound and a half to a ton of grain is recommended by Professor Riley. When used in a reasonably close room or in a nearly empty bin, one pound of the bisulphide should be evaporated for every one thousand feet of cubic space, or in a space ten by ten by ten feet, one-third of a pound in each of three shallow vessels for a space of these dimensions; for a space ten by ten by twenty feet, use two pounds in six vessels; for a room ten by twenty by twenty feet, use four pounds in twelve vessels, and so on. Make the room tight as is convenient. The vitality of the grain will not be injured in the least, nor will its edible qualities be harmed.

One point should be always borne in mind in using bisulphide of carbon, and that is its extreme inflammability; its vapor when confined is even explosive. No light nor fire should be brought into its vicinity. With care in this respect, however, it is easy and safe to handle, and it is not dangerous for a human being to inhale a reasonable amount of the vapor, in spite of its extremely offensive odor—to which, by the way, one soon becomes accustomed.

There is no need to insist, before this institute, upon the value of concert of action in many farm operations, but in no way can the results of concert of action be made of more practical benefit than in the warfare against injurious insects. In regard to this specific pest I feel certain that following the plan outlined will result in the almost complete annihilation of the loss which it annually occasions.

It may be well to add that the bisulfide of carbon treatment above outlined is efficacious not only against the so-called fly weevil, or angoumois grain moth, as it is sometimes called, but against all other insects which affect stored grain, and of these we have some five or six species in this country, all beetles in the parent stage. I may also add that this capital remedy was first suggested by Dr. C. V. Riley, in the columns of the Farmers' Review, of Chicago, in March, 1879.

In the purchase of bisulphide of carbon co-operation may be used to great advantage. It can be bought from wholesale chemists in fifty-pound cans for fifteen cents per pound. At retail it costs from twenty-five to thirty-five cents per pound. It is perhaps unnecessary to state that when not in use it should be kept in tightly-closed receptacles, in which there is as little air space as possible.

RID ELEVATOR OF WEEVIL.

Editor American Elevator and Grain Trade, issued Mar. 15, '93.—In a recent number of your journal you gave instructions how to rid an elevator of weevil. This information has saved me more than $100. I followed your instructions and my house is now free from all insects as well as mould.

Yours, E. W. K.

Now the gay and festive weevel is a living, present evil. E. W. Kruse writes to the editor from Higginsville, Mo., in a happy strain about his experience with the pest. "My grain elevator," says he, "was badly infested. I used bisulphide of carbon, and am surprised at the result; for it not only cleared out the weevil and mould but—another wonder—even the rats have left the premises."—From Roller Miller, April, 1893.

Rochester, N. Y., September 9th, '07.
Mr. Edward R. Taylor,
Penn Yan, N. Y.

Dear Sir:—Inclosed please find check for Fuma. We wish to state that the fumigation was a great success. We distributed the Fuma around in small pans and waste and poured it on the floor in some places. In the wheat and corn and oat bins we poured it on the grain. This was done on a Saturday afternoon and on opening up the mill on Monday morning nothing with life was found in the mill, and up to this date have seen no signs of them returning, consequently we believe that the Fuma not only destroyed the insects but also the eggs. We are more than pleased with our success. We are,

Very truly yours,
MACAULEY-FIEN MILLING CO.
(Geo. Fien.)

BISULPHIDE OF CARBON ROUTED THEM.

Hubbard, O., January 5. 1893.

Editor Southwestern Miller:—In 1890 and 1891 my mill was overrun with black weevils. They got into the wheat, in the flour in bins, in the flour in sacks, and in fact got everywhere except away and into the next county. After burning large quantities of sulphur and brimstone, scrubbing with whale oil soap. sprinkling with insect powder, saturating screenings bin with coal oil, and trying all the remedies suggested in and through the various milling journals without avail—as they multiplied on the face of the earth, or rather in the mill—as a last resort I purchased 100 pounds of bisulphide of carbon from Edward R. Taylor, of Cleveland, O. After following instructions to thoroughly clean up the mill, remove all bags, sacks, flour, etc., to as much as possible allow the vapor to circulate in and near their hiding places, and to make the mill as nearly air-tight as possible, I then procured 100 soup plates, and put fifty pounds in the lower story and fifty pounds in the second story, both distributions placed as near the ceilings as we could place them. This was done Saturday afternoon. When the fires were all out we filled the plates with bisulphide—being careful to keep above the fumes—and allowed no lights about. When this was done we locked the doors and did not go near till Monday morning, when we opened all the mill doors and windows to allow any remaining fumes to blow away. We then removed the plates, and on close examination not a live weevil could be found in all the mill, nor were any seen until this last spring, and then only a few. Another fifty pounds of bisulphide would have completely removed them, but as I had rented the mill I did not get any more. Now the secret of perfect success is in first getting at their haunts, which are dirty corners, screenings piles and heated wheat—clean up the dirt, remove the screenings if practicable and stir up the wheat if convenient, and then use enough of the bisulphide of carbon. Don't evaporate only fifty pounds in a place where 100 pounds are needed and expect good results. Resort to heroic treatment at the start and you will be satisfied with the results. To persons whose mills are alive with weevils—and their name is legion—we have this advice to offer: Write to Mr. Taylor and get ready to open the campaign against the insects early in the spring before they have time to hatch out the new crop, and all desirable information will be cheerfully given. Respectfully yours, A. B. SHOOK.

From Southwestern Miller, January, 1893.

BISULPHIDE OF CARBON FOR WEEVIL.

[From the American Miller of Nov. 1, 1891.]

Editor American Miller:—In my last letter I promised to give my experience with bisulphide of carbon on my crop of weevil in mitey big doses.

I cleaned up the mill on a Saturday, removed all barrels, bags, etc., where the weevil could hide, and closed the mill as airtight as possible. I procured 100 soup plates and placed fifty on the first floor filled full of the bisulphide, and fifty on the second floor, as near their haunts as possible, and closed the doors until Monday morning, when presto! change, they were nearly all gone to the happy weevil hunting grounds. I saw a few sickly live ones during the week, but even they gave up the ghost and I have not seen a weevil in two weeks.

The trouble with my use of the bisulphide of carbon before was, I did not use enough. I am satisfied that if any of my afflicted brothers will thoroughly clean up his mill and evaporate not less than 100 pounds, as I did, he can say good-bye, weevil. Eternal cleaning and bisulphide of carbon are the price of ridding your mills of the weevil. I am respectfully.

Your mitey friend,
Hubbard, O.   A. B. SHOOK.

(From Delaware College Agriculture Experiment Station.)
Bulletin No. XXI. Newark, Del.

"We have used the bisulphide of carbon on several thousand bushels of wheat infested with the granary weevil, with most excellent results."

Rochester, N. Y., Aug. 17, 1906.
Mr. E. R. Taylor, Penn Yan, N. Y.

Dear Sir: We take pleasure in informing you that we are more than satisfied with the results obtained from using "Fuma" in exterminating the Mediterranean Moth, insects, etc., and would take pleasure in recommending it, we are

Very truly yours.
MACAULEY FIEN MILLING CO.

Marion, Ohio, 6, 18, 1907.
Edward R. Taylor, Penn Yan, N. Y.

Dear Sir: Your favor of June 17th at hand and contents noted.

We have used considerable of your Fuma and find it very effective in exterminating weevil and vermin which are the pests of the miller and are pleased to recommend it to any one who is to hered in this way.   Yours respectfully,
Dic. F. H. O.   THE MARION MILLING & GRAIN CO.

Walla Walla, Washington, June 22, '07.
Edward B. Taylor, Penn Yan, N. Y.

Dear Sir: We have used about 200 gals. of your "Fuma" to good advantage. Using about 100 gal. each year we find it keeps our mill almost free from mill pests, including rats and mice. Wishing you continued success,   We remain,
DEMENT BROS. CO.

Salina, Kans., U. S. A., 6, 21, '07.
E. R. Taylor, Penn Yan, N. Y.

Dear Sir: In regard to the benefits which we have derived from the use of Bisulphide of Carbon would state that we have used considerable of this carbon and we get good results, though we find that in order to destroy all the weevil it is necessary to make two applications about a week or ten days apart. By doing this you can practically get rid of everything. Then, too, it is easier to handle than most any other kind of stuff we know as it is not so dangerous, though of course it is nothing to play with. The amount of stuff we have purchased from you shows that we fully believe in making use of it, or we certainly would have never ordered the amount of carbon we have.

Yours truly,
F. D. S.   SHELLABARGER MILL & ELE. CO.

Oriskany Falls, N. Y., June 24, 1907.
Edward R. Taylor, Penn Yan, N. Y.

Dear Sir: Please send me fifty pounds of the Fuma Carbon Bisulphide. I find there are a few of the bugs left yet, but can keep them down by the use of the Fuma once in a while.

Truly, E. S. HAMBLIN.

Covington, Va., June 17, 1907.
Mr. Edward R. Taylor.

Dear Sir: Your favor of the 15th received. We have used your Fuma some five or six different times, and the result in each case was entirely satisfactory. Yours truly,

MC ALLISTER & BELL.

Detroit, Mich., June 18, '07.
Edward R. Taylor, Penn Yan, N. Y.

Dear Sir: Please enter our order for 2,000 lbs. of Fuma (Bisulphide of Carbon) for July shipment. We will be returning what empty drums we have soon.

We have used this insecticide for the past twelve years in large quantities and consider it indispensable as it enables us to keep the insects that infest seeds within reasonable bounds. Please acknowledge receipt of the order and oblige,

JEROME B. RICE SEED CO.

Monticello, Ind., June 17, 1907.
Mr. Edward R. Taylor, Penn Yan, N. Y.

Dear Sir: We have been using your Bisulphide of Carbon for several years to rid our mill and elevator of insects. When properly applied we find that it does the work in a very satisfactory manner. Without this or something to take its place we could not operate our plant. Yours very truly,

LOUGHRY BROS. MILLING AND GRAIN CO.

Wonewoc, Wis., June 24, '07.
E. R. Taylor.

Dear Sir: We fumigated our mill about two weeks ago and have not seen any weevil or moths since nor any rats or mice. As soon as we can get the grain out of our elevator we will want to fumigate again which will be along in August.

Very truly yours,

WONEWOC MILL CO.

Edward R. Taylor, Penn Yan, N. Y.

Dear Sir: Enclosed please find B-L. for three empty drums returned to you today for which please give us credit.

We wish to state that we used the three drums in one large steel tank which had in it 19,000 bushels of wheat which was so full of weevil that it looked as though they would eat it up in spite of all we could do in the way of shifting. After using this Fuma we have been unable to find any weevil at all except in about 1,000 bushels in bottom of bin.

Yours truly,

FARMERSVILLE MILL AND LIGHT CO.,
E. W. STEWART, Mgr.

New Orleans, La., 6, 20, '07.
Mr. E. R. Taylor, Penn Yan, N. Y.

Dear Sir: Replying to your favor of the 17th inst. beg to advise that we used some of your chemicals last year and found them to be everything that you claim for them.

Yours truly,
NEW ORLEANS MILLING CO.

GRAIN DESTROYERS.

Weevils are making themselves so obnoxious in this country that experts of the Department of Agriculture are now engaged in making a special study of them. Every year they destroy many millions of dollars' worth of stored cereals in granaries and elevators. In fact, the question how to fight them is one of serious and growing economic importance. Strange to say, very little scientific attention has been directed to these insects up to date, and not much is known about them. It is reckoned that they cause an annual loss of over $1,000,000 in Texas alone, and in 1893 the corn crop of Alabama was damaged by them to the extent of $1,670,000.

There are about forty species of these insects, some of which are beetles and other moths. Nearly all of them are assisted emigrants, having been imported from abroad in cargoes of grain. In this manner they have been distributed by commerce to all parts of the world. Their native homes are in the tropics. Having become domesticated after a fashion by men, they depend in colder countries entirely upon him for subsistence, the beetles passing the whole of their lives and propagating their kind, generation after generation, in his grain bins.

The damage they do is well-nigh incalculable. Three species actually live in the kernels, while the others feed on starchy contents. Grain infested by them is unfit for human consumption, and has been known to cause serious illness. It is poisonous to horses and is not wholesome even for swine. Poultry, however, find it palatable and nutritious. The moths, especially, are so prolific that the progeny of a single pair in a twelvemonth will number many thousands, capable of destroying several tons of grain. Fortunately, the increase of these pests is checked to some extent by natural enemies, among which are spiders that inhabit mills and granaries. In the fields they are preyed upon by birds and bats.

One of the worst of these insects is the familiar "granary weevil," which is mentioned in the Georgics of Virgil. Its ravages made it known long before the Christian era. It is native to the region of the Mediterranean. Having been domesticated for so long a time, it has lost use of its wings. The female punctures the kernel with her snout and inserts an egg, from which is hatched a little worm that lives in the hull and feeds on the starchy interior. This species devotes special attention to wheat, corn and barley, and it is also very partial to the chicken-pea, which is much cultivated as a vegetable in the tropics.

Quite as bad as this beetle is a moth that comes from the Mediterranean region also. The larva, which is known in the United States as the "fly weevil," does most injury to corn and wheat. In six months grain infested by it loses 40 per cent.

in weight and 75 per cent. of its starchy matter. Incidentally, it is rendered totally unfit for food, and bread made from wheat infested by the insect is said to have caused an epidemic recently in France. The pest was noticed in North Carolina as early as 1728, and since that time it has spread all over the South. The mother moth lays her eggs in standing grain, and after a few days the little caterpillars are hatched out and burrow into the kernels.

Another wicked imported bug is the "rice weevil." It originated in India, whence it has been distributed by commerce all over the world. At present it does as much harm as any other known insect, being a serious pest in the Southern States. In the tropics generally it does enormous damage. Formerly when long voyages were necessary in importing grain from the East, it frequently destroyed whole cargoes, having plenty of time to multiply. The adult beetles of this species cause much trouble in store houses and groceries by invading boxes of crackers, cakes, yeast cakes and macaroni and barrels and bins of flour and meal. They can subsist for months on sugar, and sometimes they burrow into ripening peaches and grapes.

A new grain destroyer has recently attracted attention in this country, and has earned for itself the title of "scourge of the flour mill." It is the "Mediterranean flour moth." The caterpillars spin webs which make the flour clotted and lumpy, so that the machinery in the mills becomes clogged and has to be stopped for a considerable time, the result being a loss of thousands of dollars in large establishments. The larvae prefer flour or meal, but they flourish also in bran, prepared cereal food and crackers. Nearly related to this species is another, known as the "Indian meal moth." It devours pretty nearly everything, feeding on grain and farinaceous products of all kinds, dried fruits, seeds and nuts of various sorts, condiments, roots and herbs. It even attacks dried insects in cabinets, and is said to devour sugar, jellies and yeast cakes. Occasionally it is troublesome in beehives, eating the honey. In short, it is an all-round nuisance. The caterpillars so often found in dried apples, currants, raisins and English walnuts are the offspring of the Indian meal moth.

During the past year two little beetles, popularly known as "flour weevils" have caused much alarm among millers, flour and feed dealers, grocers and dealers in patent foods. For a long time they have been familiar in Europe as enemies of meal, flour, grain and other stored products and even as pests in museums. Though they live in grain, they do most damage to flour and to patent articles of diet containing starch. The eggs are deposited in the flour, and these and the young caterpillars, being minute and pale in color, are not noticed. But, after the flour has been sealed up in barrels or boxes for a while, the adult beetles make their appearance and ruin the food material. Furthermore, the insects have a very offensive smell, the presence of a few specimens sufficing to impart a disagreeable and offensive odor to the substance infested by them. They attack snuff, orris-root, baking powder, rice, chaff, red pepper and graham flour.

This subject is considered of such importance that considerable space was devoted to it in the Year Book of the Department of Agriculture for 1895. The remarks made therein are based upon recent study of weevils and their habits by Mr. F. H

Chittenden, of the Bureau of Entomology. Farmers are informed that the best remedy for such mischief is Bisulfide of Carbon, which may be applied in moderately tight bins by simply pouring the liquid into shallow pans or on bits of cotton waste and distributing them about on the surface of the grain. The stuff rapidly evaporates, and the vapor being heavier than air, descends and permeates the mass of grain, killing all insects, as well as rats and mice which it may contain. This method may be adopted to great advantage in elevators, which may be closed for the purpose over Sunday. The Bisulfide of Carbon is very explosive, and to breathe much of the vapor is dangerous to human beings, but it is perfectly safe with careful use.

A COPY OF J. C. DANIELS AND CO.'S TESTIMONIAL.

We have used Bisulfide of Carbon for three years and have found it by far the greatest aid in ridding our plant of insect pests that we have ever tried. It is a deadly enemy to rats, weevil or any breathing insect.

While these pests may return yet a single combat in which Bisulfide is the weapon of defense is sufficient to persuade any pest named that 'tis better to dwell in some far off country. We regard it as one of the essential helps.

J. C. DANIELS & CO.

Middletown, Ind., Dec. 12, 1894.

HANDLING WEEVILY WHEAT.

The rapidity with which weevils breed makes it necessary that prompt attention be given to grain in which they are discovered. Some idea of the rate of increase may be had from the statements of David Hooper, curator of the Indian Museum, Calcutta, who has made some experiments in connection with the ravages of weevils in stored wheat. In the course of his research he found that the weevils introduced into the wheat at the beginning of the period had multiplied sixty times. The counting of an average 100 grains showed that 65 per cent. had been attacked by the pest, while the wheat had lost 26 per cent. of its weight in three months.

While fumigation with bisulphide of carbon is the only sure method of exterminating weevils, it is possible to minimize their destructive work by handling the grain. This might properly be termed an emergency measure and consists in screening the grain on a sieve that will retain the wheat and allow the weevils to drop through, at the same time subjecting the grain to a strong air blast, which will lift out the insects.

The principal objection to this method is that it fails to destroy the eggs or larvae in the wheat grains. These can only be reached by the proper application of bisulphide of carbon. While the latter may be poured or sprayed over the infested grain, the best results are obtained by allowing the liquid to evaporate and the fumes to penetrate the grain. The bins in which the grain is treated should be fairly tight and the bisulphide of carbon should be placed in shallow pans on the top of the grain. The liquid volatilizes rapidly and, being heavier than the air, sinks down into the grain, killing all insects and vermin present.

It should be remembered that the bisulphide is highly inflammable and no fire of any kind should be allowed in the mill until the fumes have entirely passed away.—American Miller, December, 1907.

HOW TO KILL CORN WEEVILS.

The fall of 1893 we made applications of Carbon Bisulfide to corn in shuck and to corn with shuck taken off to kill the large number of weevils that were in the corn at the time.

This material is a foul-smelling liquid which evaporates at ordinary temperatures and is highly inflammable. We placed a pint of this fluid every three feet in the several bins of corn on November 11th.

On December 10th, we opened the corn and found all the weevils dead that were in the shucked corn, all the liquid evaporated from the cans. The corn in the shuck still had a few living weevils in it, but by far the greater part were dead. On February 10th following, we again inspected the corn and found all weevils dead in both kinds of corn. No fresh weevils had entered and thousands of dead ones testified to the efficient method of treatment.

J. H. CONNELL,

Texas Experiment Station.

LOSS FROM GRAIN WEEVILS IN TEXAS.

A Texas correspondent of *Insect Life* writes: "For many years in succession I had my corn in the bin more or less ruined by weevils. From my own experience in this line, and what I know from other sources, I should judge that there is *an annual loss of over a million dollars from weevils in Texas alone.*

Last fall, in putting up my corn, I placed two open bottles containing Bisulfide of Carbon about four feet apart on the floor of the bin. The mouths of these bottles were covered with a single layer of cheese cloth, and each bottle covered with an old broken box. The corn was thrown on these boxes and the bin filled to its utmost capacity.

The result of this experiment was highly successful. What live weevils were admitted from the field were destroyed and none further appeared. Thus, at a cost of fifty cents, with very little trouble, I effectually protected about 500 bushels of corn against the weevils. Another feature about this experiment is that I have noticed neither mouse nor rat in the bin, nor any traces of them, which was not the case before, for in previous years they, too, had done great damage to the corn.—*Published in American Elevator and Grain Trade. Aug. 15, '92.*

The report of Experiment Station at Newark, Delaware, in *Bulletin* No. 21, says: "We have used the Bisulfide of Carbon on several thousand bushels of wheat infested with the granary weevil with most excellent results."

CEREALLELLA, OLIV.

This insect has caused much damage to stored grain in this state for many years. At the Station during the past year it has been exceedingly destructive, wheat put into the barns in June being entirely destroyed by September. It attacks wheat and corn especially, but other grains are by no means exempt.

DESCRIPTION.

The imago or mature form of this insect is a small moth, shown at c in Fig. 1. (See cut on front cover.) The wings expand slightly over one-half inch in length, and the antennæ are nearly as long as the body, tapering at the extremity. The body and forewings are of a light gray color and have a soft shiny appearance; the hindwings are of a darker hue than the forewings, narrow, and tapering to a point at the outer ends. The outer posterior extremities of the fore-wings bear light gray colored scales which are thickest near the tip of the wings. The fringe surrounding the hind-wings is of the same color as the wings, being shortest at the outer anterior extremity (when the wings are outspread as in the figure) and longest at the inner posterior edge. The underside of the wings is much darker than the upper side. The legs are slightly darker than the body, the posterior pair being quite hairy and each bearing two prominent spurs.

The insects reproduce so rapidly that it takes but a short time to destroy the grain when stored. In Fig. 2 is shown an ear of corn from which the moths have escaped. The nutritious portion of the grain is entirely eaten, and infested grain will not germinate.—*Alabama Exp. Station Bulletin 61. Auburn, Ala.*

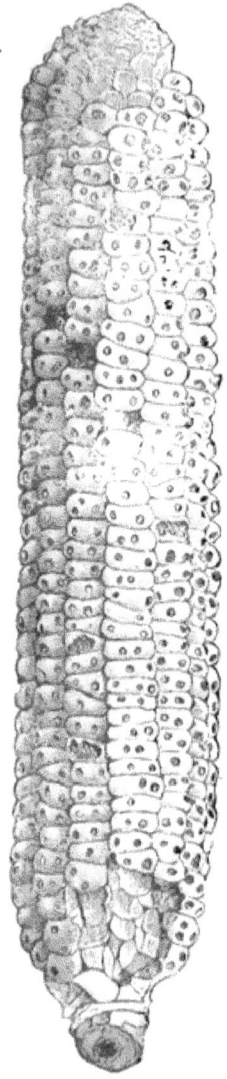

KILL THE WEEVIL BEFORE TAKING INFESTED GRAIN INTO YOUR MILL.

Bluffton. O., Aug. 15, 1896.

Edward R. Taylor, Cleveland, O.

Dear Sir:—You will please find enclosed check for $2.40 for Bisulfide of Carbon shipped me a few days ago. I gave the preparation a good test on one thousand bushels of wheat, in a car that was very badly infested with weevil. Twenty-four hours proved the test. At the end of that time the weevil had all gone to the forever beyond. I can cheerfully recommend it to anyone who may wish to use it faor the destruction of vermin in grain.

Yours very truly, JULIAN DORIOT.

GOOD FOR BUGS AND RHEUMATISM.

It seems as if that trusty servant of the miller, bisulphide of carbon, is to enlarge its sphere of usefulness. A doctor says in a recent publication: "I suffered from sciatica and rheumatism the torments of hell for six weeks, and was cured in less than three minutes by rubbing in from hip to heel half an ounce of carbon bisulphide. Give it to suffering humanity. A gentleman from Canada called to see me, saw my intense sufferings, and told me a wealthy man spent a large fortune in trying to get cured of rheumatism, and that ten cents' worth of the above cured him. Like a drowning man grasping at a straw, I tried it and was well before I got dressed."

It doesn't cost much to try it and we pass it along to the miller for what it is worth.—American Miller, October 1, 1900.

Wahoo, Neb., August 20, 1907.

Edw. R. Taylor, Esq.,
Penn Yan, N. Y.

Dear Sir: Enclosed please find N. Y. draft for $8.50, also R. R. receipt for two drums returned. Large drum of this shipment and small drum from last shipment, freight prepaid on them. The Fuma will do the work every time.

Yours truly,
WAHOO MILL CO.

INSECTS IN STORED GRAIN.

Bellevue, Ohio.

Have you a recipe to kill weevils and insects in wheat? If so, kindly publish it. We have seen it in your paper but cannot remember it. K. G.

Reply.—For about every ton of grain, place in the bin one pound of Bisulfide of Carbon. Simply make excavations in the surface and pour in the Bisulfide, which is a fluid, then draw back the grain, level off the surface and cover with blankets or similar objects, to keep the fumes down. The fumes will penetrate the grain and kill everything among it in the way of insects. This is an explosive and must not be used near where there is fire of any sort.—Ohio Farmer, Aug. 13, 1896.

For a two-story 30x40-foot building use not less than 100 pounds. Double amount if badly infested.

HIGGINSVILLE, MO., May 4, 1893.

EDWARD R. TAYLOR, ESQ., Cleveland, O.

Dear Sir:—As I wrote you some time ago, my elevator was badly infested with weevil and also full of rats. I sent to you for fifty pounds of Bisulfide and used it according to your directions. I had at the time about twenty-five hundred to three thousand bushels of wheat in the house; this was last fall some time. I am now milling this wheat, and if there is any sign of weevil or rats, neither I nor any one else can find them. I simply poured the Bisulfide in the corners of the bin, about one quart at a place, making a gallon to about one thousand bushels. The top of the wheat was about twenty to thirty feet above the ground floor, and the stuff must have gone down and cleaned out the rats for they are gone, and this is a ratty neighborhood. E. W. KRUSE.

IT CLEARED THE MICE OUT OF OUR FLOUR HOUSE.

MT. CARMEL, ILLS., May 4, 1893.

EDWARD R. TAYLOR:

Dear Sir:—Enclosed find five dollars, amount of your bill. That is the stuff. It cleaned the mice out of our flour house. We simply opened the can and let it set in the house and it killed all young mice and drove the old ones away. Send us another can same size as last. Yours respectfully, THE J. M. SHIRK CO.

In subsequent letters they say: "There is about one-third of the Bisulfide left in the can and by shaking it up once a day it seems to have the desired effect. We only used it in our flour houses but intend to use second can in mill, which is full of mill insects.

We never had any fear of fire from the carbon, but of course used good common sense and cautioned all our men when they opened the flour house. There are no insects or worms of any kind in our flour house and we think it was your stuff that keeps them out. We move the can from one place to another every day or so.

You may use our letter as every miller and farmer should have a stock of it on hand. It certainly is great stuff.

Yours respectfully, THE J. M. SHIRK CO.

I do not advise the use of less than 100 pounds even for a moderately small mill. If too little is used, the goods and the work are lost, and relief not obtained; if more than is necessary is used, the excess only is lost and the work done. Spraying is not advisable, as the bulk of the liquid is absorbed into the wood and is given out so slowly that it does not produce a *death atmosphere*. Do not use old fruit cans, they are too deep and the vapor cannot get out of them quick enough.

BISULFIDE FOR MOLES.

Richmond Hill, L. I., July 9, 1896.

Edward R. Taylor.

Dear Sir:—Will you please send me the little pamphlet and slips regarding the liquid "Fuma?" We have used it for moles and found it excellent.

Richmond Hill, Aug. 3, 1896.

Mr. Taylor.

Dear Sir:—In answer to yours of July 29, asking how I used the Bisulfide of Carbon for moles, would say that I followed your directions; that is, when there were indications of moles to be seen, would dig until I found the run, then insert a ball of cotton thoroughly saturated with the "Fuma" in each opening, then pack the earth firmly over the opening I had made. As these little animals have so many turns to their paths, I was not satisfied by putting the first balls of cotton in. I would follow the run and put some more well saturated cotton in the same as the first, always being careful to pack the earth firmly over the opening when I had placed the "Fuma." I followed one run until I had put in eight balls of saturated cotton, which means that I opened the run in four places and put in a ball of cotton in each side of the opening. I always think that anything that is worth doing at all is worth doing well, and we were about discouraged, as the moles were fast destroying a lawn we were anxious to save. When I saw in a paper (I cannot name the paper) mention of Bisulfide of Carbon, I immediately wrote you and was determined to give your "Fuma" a good trial, and am very glad I did. We have found that borers in trees that are too far in to be cut out, can be killed by the "Fuma," using a squirt can, then filling the hole with putty or a little mud. Yours truly, A. B. SWAN.

DEATH TO OUR FOES.

A. B. Johnson, of Cottage, N. Y., asks us to publish the following as an answer to numerous inquiries he has received in regard to the use of Bisulfide of Carbon. He says: "It is as safe to handle as coal oil, excepting when too near a fire; it is sure death to all kinds of pests, from smallest to the largest. To destroy woodchucks, hold a ball of cotton batting or anything dry that will absorb the fluid quickly, over the entrance of the animal's den and pour one or two tablespoonfuls of the Bisulfide of Carbon on it. Put it in the den two or three feet, then fill the hole with a piece of turf, 18 inches down, and hoe on dirt and tramp it down; if it is a very complicated den, or there is a large family, use more on other outlets and close them all; from two to three pounds will kill 100 woodchucks, and is an easy day's work for a part-grown boy. I used it last summer freely; it cost me 12 cents per pound. I had to send to Edward R. Taylor, Manufacturing Chemist, Cleveland, Ohio, to get it, but its value to me was more than five dollars per pound."—Grape Belt, Dunkirk, New York.

I have always had my share of woodchucks, and I never could get rid of them until last season. I got an ounce of Bisulfide of Carbon, used one-half on three burrows and, in about three hours, all three had been dug out. I used the other half where an old one had young; the next morning I dug out the hole and found them dead. A neighbor joined with me and we got 20 pounds from Cleveland, at 12 cents per pound; one pound is enough for fifty, and not one has ever dug out of the hundreds that we have treated, unless there was some opening that we missed. Pour from one to two spoonfuls on anything that will absorb the stuff, push it into the hole three feet, push down a sod nearly to it, hoe on earth and tramp down. Treat all main outlets the same, and next summer one will be puzzled to find the place.—A. B. J., The Rural New Yorker, Aug. 15, 1896.

FUMA CARBON BISULPHIDE.

A word in regard to Fuma Carbon Bisulphide. In the early summer of 1887, I first sent this grade to Isaiah Lightner for killing prairie dogs; he was greatly delighted with his success, and, though not knowing why, found it superior for this purpose to that he had bought before he knew of my article. Since that time I have had numerous opportunities of knowing that this grade is many times better than I had supposed.

The first order I had from the Michigan miller referred to by Prof. Cooke in bulletin 58, I sent part of his order of "Fuma" and part the commercial grade. I did this with considerable hesitation, as I feared it might taint his goods. But his next and all subsequent orders were for the strongest goods I could send, and you notice he said, "You can throw it right on to flour and it soon will vaporize and the flour is in no wise injured." Other millers have testified to the same fact and not a single one has ever advised me of any injury to any mill product. So I think millers can assuredly rest upon that as a settled question.

Provincial Fruit Inspector's Office,
Vancouver, B. C., Aug. 28, 1906.

* * * We are likely to use a great deal of this most valuable insecticide; at present are using it for fumigating Japanese infected rice, and we are succeeding beyond my highest expectation * * *.

Sept. 15, 1906. * * * We are having uninterrupted success with the Fuma * * *.

Aug. 26, 1907. * * * We are now fumigating two hundred tons of Japanese rice at Victoria * * *. * * * Please send forward ten fifty-pound drums of Fuma * * *.

THOMAS CUNNINGHAM,
Provincial Fruit Inspector.

USES OF BISULPHIDE OF CARBON.

For making a water-proof Cement for Shoemakers and others, by dissolving Gutta-Percha.

With Chloride of Sulphur, for vulcanizing India-rubber and linseed oil goods.

Is the best solvent for India-rubber; dissolves Gum, Dammar, Mastic, Ammoniacum, etc., used for making varnishes.

For extracting oil from seeds, wool, bones and aromatic substances, perfumes, etc.

For the destruction of Rats, Gophers, Prairie Dogs and other burrowing animals, by pouring it into their holes with a funnel and lead or rubber pipe, 2 or 3 feet long; for Noxious Insects, such as Weevils, Moths, Ants, etc. For Weevils, ½ ounce per ton of grain in a closed bin is sufficient. Also by seedsmen for killing insects in seeds, and Zoologists, in place of chloroform, for killing specimens without mutilation, its vapor having the same effect on animal life.

For killing Phyloxera on grape vines, by injecting into the ground near the roots.

For fumigating mail matter, etc., from infected districts, and by physicians for disinfecting their clothing after exposure to infectious diseases. The liquid itself is used for all these purposes, the same as for grain.

For fumigating houses in time of infectious diseases, especially Diphtheria, by burning in an iron ladle, or other suitable vessel, and carrying through the rooms of the house.

For preserving Meat, Fruits and other perishable articles.

Gun Cotton treated with it in a closed vessel, loses its explosive power, burning quietly and without explosion, until after exposure to the air and the evaporation of the Bisulphide of Carbon, when it regains its explosive quality without loss.

Used in Silver Plating to give a bright and brilliant surface at once.

Water dissolves one and one-half per cent. of Bisulphide of Carbon, making one of the best disinfectants known.

For making Chloroform and Tetrachloride of Carbon.

For making Viscose from wood pulp, from which is made Viscose artificial silk of the most beautiful character.

(Abstracts from Farmer's Bulletin No. 145. Pages 78 to 95 inclusive.)

CARBON BISULPHID AS AN INSECTICIDE.

FIRST USE AS AN INSECTICIDE.

So far as the writer can learn, the use of carbon bisulphid as an insecticide was made in 1856 and 1857 by M. Doyere, who demonstrated that a small amount of the liquid poured into a pit of corn or barley would kill all the weevils and their eggs; that this chemical agent did not alter at all the quality of the grain; that it left only a slight odor, which was not, however, persistent, but disappeared promptly upon the exposure of the grain to the free air. Since that time its use has steadily increased and it is now generally recognized as one of the most useful insecticides.

APPLICABILITY TO VARIOUS INSECTS.

Carbon bisulphid is applicable to a large number of insect pests living under very different conditions, which, therefore, require different modes of application. These insects can be divided into groups, according to certain similarities of their habits of life or of their habitats. The members of each group have been found to be susceptible to practically the same mode of treatment with such minor variations as the individual life histories may require for greatest effectiveness. In a general way we may say that carbon bisulphid is applicable only where its vapor can be more or less confined. Its field of usefulness is among those insects which can not be reached through poisoning their food and those that are very difficult to reach with contact insecticides by spraying. Such insects are found both indoors and out of doors, and the general methods of treatment in these two environments must necessarily vary considerably.

DIFFUSION OF THE VAPOR.

This vapor diffuses through the air very rapidly and must, therefore, be closely confined in order to maintain a sufficient proportion of it in the atmosphere to prove fatal to insect life. It tends most strongly to spread outward and downward on account of its being so heavy, and, though it will gradually work upward, its greatest density will be at the lowest levels. The usual calculation is to employ one pound of liquid carbon bisulphid to each 1,000 cubic feet of space treated, whether for the treatment of insects in buildings or for insects in the ground. This amount gives an atmosphere, if confined to that space, composed approximately of 1 part in 90 of carbon bisulphid vapor, which, as we shall see, is a fatal strength in a short time. However, where the atmosphere cannot be absolutely confined and there is considerable opportunity for the vapor to escape, it is frequently necessary to apply from two to four times that amount, under circumstances where there is no danger of killing plant life.

INSECTICIDAL POWER.

In 1876 two French investigators, Cornu and Mouillefert, performed a series of experiments to determine the insecticidal power of carbon bisulphid vapor. They were working primarily upon the grape Phylloxera, but, in addition to that insect, they experimented with caterpillars, butterflies, cicadas, wasps and plant-lice. In a series of five large flasks they produced an atmosphere composed of 1 part of carbon bisulphid vapor to 12, 30, 60, 120 and 180 parts of air. Within each of these flasks grape roots bearing the Phylloxera were confined for twenty-four hours, at the end of which time the insects were dead in each case. In other experiments in which all of the previously mentioned insects were used it was found that in an atmosphere composed of 1 part carbon bisulphid vapor to 90 parts air, all insects perished in a few seconds, and that an atmosphere composed of 1 part of carbon bisulphid vapor to 254 parts of air was fatal in one and one-fourth hours. The same result is therefore attained by a small proportion of the vapor acting through a long time as by a large proportion acting for a short time.

HOW PUT UP AND COST.

Carbon bisulphid is put up in tight cans or iron drums holding from 1 to 50 pounds. It may be purchased in small quantities of any druggist, at from 25 to 35 cents per pound; but if any considerable quantity is to be used, it is much better to buy of some wholesale druggist, or, better still, direct from the manufacturers. In the latter way it is shipped in 50 pound cans or drums at 10 cents per pound, with an additional charge for the drums, which are returnable at the purchase price; but all freight charges are paid by the buyer.

USES OF CARBON BISULPHID.

PHYLLOXERA TREATMENT.

It is for insects living underground especially that this insecticide fills a need which has not yet been equally well met by any other. By far its largest use in insecticidal work has been in France against the grape Phylloxera—a little plant-louse living mainly upon the roots of that vine. This insect is a native of the United States, and from here was introduced into France about 1859 upon imported vines. As is the rule with insect pests, this plant-louse proved to be far more destructive to the vines in France than it has been in this country. In 1863 its first injuries were manifest, and in less than ten years it had multiplied so enormously there and spread so widely that it was feared that vine growing in France was doomed. This insect's connection with the deterioration and death of the vines was not known until 1868, when it was proven by a French scientist.

This insecticide was first applied to the Phylloxera in 1859 by Baron Paul Thenard. Unfortunately in attempting to force the fumes to the necessary depth to kill the insects he also killed his vines by the over-dose. Later experiments gave better results. In 1873 the use of carbon bisulphid rapidly increased until over 200,000 acres were receiving annual treatment. Treatment had to be repeated for three years before the vines regained their normal condition.

This use of carbon bisulphid for the Phylloxera was the beginning of its underground use. The following is a summary of the principal conclusions reached by many experimenters in the course of years of work against this little root louse:

Diffusion of the vapor in the soil.—Upon being introduced into the soil at some depth below the surface the liquid evaporates as it does in the open air, only much more slowly. The vapor tends to diffuse through all the air spaces of the soil. It thus produces an atmosphere which is fatal to all insects living within its reach. The rapidity of evaporation, the extent of diffusion, and the persistence of the vapor in the soil vary widely in soils of varying characters and conditions, so no one rule of application can be employed in all cases, and it thus becomes necessary to understand the influence of various factors that proper allowance may be made for them and the destruction of the insects attained without injuring the plants.

Moisture.—Carbon bisulphid evaporates more rapidly in a warm, dry, sandy soil, and the persistence of the vapor is also shortest in such soil. In fact it diffuses so rapidly that most insects will survive an ordinary dose; and if the dose is increased so as to kill the insects, it is likely to kill the vines as well. The treatment cannot be successfully applied on such a soil in its dry condition. On the other hand, diffusion is slowest in heavy, wet, clay soil; and, when such soil is saturated with water, it is almost entirely prevented. Moisture lowers the temperature and decreases the permeability of the soil; it also prevents the evaporation of the liquid, and thus retards diffusion. Between these two extremes there is a medium condition of moisture which is most favorable for treatment.

Character of soil.—Sandy soils permit an even but too rapid diffusion of the vapor. Rocky soils are not of even texture, and naturally the vapors follow the lines of least resistance. Heavy clay soils, when very dry, are usually much broken by cracks and fissures, which may run from the surface to a considerable depth. Through such fissures the vapor escapes rapidly without permeating the soil to any extent, and its insecticidal value is therefore slight. But when such a soil is well moistened it is even in texture and very favorable to treatment.

Depth of soil.—The depth of the soil is an important factor in determining how much carbon bisulphid must be used for a given area. If the soil is shallow and the subsoil very dense and impervious, it is evident that much less liquid will be required to produce a death atmosphere than will be needed in a soil of much greater depth. In soils of the same character and condition the amount needed will be proportional to the permeable depth of the soil. In heavy, compact soils increase the number of injections and diminish the dose; in light, deep, permeable soils decrease the number of holes and increase the dose.

Amount to use.—In field experiments with the grape, using plain carbon bisulphid in "quite fresh" soil, vines were found to withstand 105 c. v. of carbon bisulphid (4.4 ounces, nearly), divided equally among 3 holes placed about 16 inches from the base of the vine and at a depth of about 20 inches; but 180 c. c. (7½ ounces) proved fatal to the vines. In a warmer, drier, more shallow soil a dose of 90 c. c. per vine, similarly placed, proved fatal. After considerable rain, when the ground was quite wet, a vine withstood 260 c. c. of carbon bisulphid, and some vines are said to have withstood 400 c. c.

Conditions favorable to treatment.—The treatment should never be applied for some time after plowing or cultivating, as a firm, compact, moist surface is much more favorable to the retention of the vapor. For the same reason about fifteen days should be allowed after treatment before cultivation is resumed. If the soil is either very wet or very dry, treatment should be withheld. To be in the most favorable condition for treatment, the soil should be quite moist and moderately permeable, with a firm, even surface, well compacted by rain and having a depth of at least 8 inches.

Extent of diffusion.—The extent of diffusion of the vapor determines the distance apart at which the injections must be made in order to reach all parts of the soil evenly and effectively. This varies considerably with the amount of the dose, the temperature and humidity of the soil, and other conditions. It has been found more satisfactory to employ smaller and more frequent doses rather than a few large ones. A dose of 5 or 6 grams (1·5 to 1·4 ounce) is believed to be thoroughly effective through a radius from 12 to 20 inches, though it may permeate much farther than that. The general rule is to make 3 injections per square meter (1 1·5 square yards, nearly) in light soils and 4 injections in heavy soils. The arrangement of the holes must necessarily vary more or less, according to the system of planting. They should be at regular intervals, however, so as to cover the ground evenly, and never nearer than 1 foot to the base of the vine. It must be remembered that to be effective all the ground must be treated, and not merely those places where the presence of the enemy is proven by its injuries.

Repeated treatment.—On account of the liability of injuring the vines it has been found best to make the treatment in two small applications, separated by an interval of from six to ten days. This decreases the density of the vapor, but continues its action for a much longer time. It removes the danger of injuring the vines, and gives even better results upon the insects than would be obtained by one large dose. The total amount of carbon bisulphid to be used should be divided into as many equal parts as there are injections to be made. The holes for the second treatment should be intermediate between those for the first.

Depth of the holes.—The depth of the holes depends somewhat upon the depth and permeability of the soil, the average depth being about 1 foot. A depth of 16 inches is desirable upon deep or very permeable soil.

Season of application.—Treatment may be applied at any season of the year; but, as it is followed by a slight check in growth, it should not be applied either at the flowering or fruiting season, as the check would injure the crop most at those seasons. The injury to the vines results from the killing of the tender, fibrous, feeding roots. It would therefore be better to apply the treatment before these roots have started much—that is, early in spring—or after they have become hardened—that is, after fruitage in the fall. The condition of the soil usually favors the spring treatment, and the condition of the insect is said to make it more susceptible at that time. Spring, therefore, appears to be the most favorable season.

Amount to use per acre.—Two entirely different objects may be had in treatment: First, to stamp out entirely and surely all traces of the pest upon its first appearance in a vineyard, or when desiring to reset, regardless of the life vines; second, to control the pest in such a way as to prevent its multiplication while continuing the culture of the vineyard. The first is called the extinction treatment; the second, cultural treatment. The method of application is the same in each case, but the amount of the dose differs. To secure extinction, it is usual to apply about 300 grams (10 ounces, nearly) per vine, using 150 grams in each of two applications ten or twelve days apart. This is said to kill ninety-nine out of every hundred vines. In cultural treatment the amount of the liquid to be used varies, according to the conditions previously described, from 140 to 265 pounds per acre.

Instruments for application.—One of the principal difficulties in the first use of carbon bisulphid was to force the vapors to the desired depth. When first used below the surface, it was poured into holes formed by driving an iron bar with a maul. The demand for a more convenient, accurate and rapid working instrument was soon met by the invention of the pal-injector by M. Gastine. This instrument was later improved by M. Vermorel, and it fills the need admirably. The carbon bisulphid is placed in a large chamber, from which an outlet leads down through a series of valves, so adjusted that the amount of each discharge can be exactly regulated as desired, and opens near the tip of a pointed bar. The instrument is forced into the ground by the handle and the pressure of the foot upon a spur to a depth of about 1 foot; the central plunger is then pressed down and the desired amount of the liquid is discharged; the instrument is withdrawn, and the hole closed with the foot, or, as is usual in extensive work, another workman follows with a rammer, with which the holes are closed and the soil at the same time is firmly compacted. It is said that two men working together in this way can make between 2,000 and 3,000 injections per day. One acre will require on the average from 10,000 to 12,000 holes.

Plows have been invented which facilitate considerably the application, but it cannot be made as deeply as with the injectors, on account of the interference of the roots. If such a plow is used, about one-fourth to one-third more of the carbon bisulphid will be required, on account of its nearness to the surface. The liquid is ejected from the machine with so much force that it becomes separated into fine drops, thus facilitating rapid evaporation. Soil is then drawn up over the liquid and compacted by the machine. Slight explosions occasionally are produced during application, especially in stony soils, by sparks caused by the steel striking against stones, but they are by no means serious.

Retarding evaporation.—Mixtures of carbon bisulphid with other substances designed to retard evaporation have been made, and the pure liquid has been used by putting it up in gelatin capsules, which allow a slow vaporation; but as these methods have not given as good results as the use of the pure liquid they will not be discussed in detail.

Many of the foregoing statements regarding the treatment of Phylloxera apply equally well to the treatment of other insects living underground.

TREATMENT FOR ROOT MAGGOTS.

Carbon bisulphid has been more or less successfully used for the cabbage root maggot ever since ... ...en Prof. A. J. Cook experimented with it with such success that he began to recommend it. There is no doubt that its efficacy varies considerably with the nature of the soil, and there is equally little doubt that many of the failures which have been reported in its use have been due very largely to improper or too tardy application. If the liquid comes in contact with the roots, it will undoubtedly prove fatal to the plant, but a considerable amount of the vapor will do no harm. If the remedy is delayed until the plants are badly wilted, it is very likely that they will not recover, even though the enemy be killed, but their death cannot fairly be attributed to the carbon bisulphid. Some growers who have tested it thoroughly state that it will work on clay or sand without injuring the plants. It has been found fatal to the pupae as well as the larvae. Mr. M. V. Slingerland, of the Cornell University Agricultural Experiment Station, investigated the subject in 1894[*] and his "experiments demonstrated that when properly applied the substance was sure death to the insects and did not injure the plants."

[*]See Bul. No. 78, Cornell University Experiment Station.

McGowen injector.—Some instrument was needed to facilitate its application, as the French pal-injectors are too heavy and too expensive. To fill this need, the McGowen injector was produced. This very convenient little instrument could be adapted to nearly all of our uses of carbon bisulphid for underground insects, but the writer has been informed by Mr. McGowen that the demand for it has been so small that he has discontinued its manufacture.

Method of application.—Whatever the instrument used, the treatment should be made in practically the same way. The hole should start 3 or 4 inches from the stem of the plant and run down obliquely to a point a little below the roots, where the liquid is deposited. The hole is then closed with earth and compacted by pressure of the foot. The dose required varies from a teaspoonful for each small plant to a tablespoonful for large plants (4 teaspoonfuls equal 1 tablespoonful equal 1 fluid ounce approximately). One injection will be sufficient if made in time, but if delayed too long nothing can save the plant. The conditions of the soil noted under Phylloxera treatment will have practically the same influence in this case.

There appears to be no reason why a similar method of treatment may not be equally effective against such other insects as the grape root-worm (Fidia viticida) and the peach borer (Sanninoidea exitiosa), especially on young trees, where the borer usually works just beneath the surface of the ground.

DESTRUCTION OF ANTS.

Carbon bisulphid is the best remedy known for the destruction of ants, which are frequently great nuisances to farmers and gardeners. With a little careful observation most of the common house ants, except the little red house ants, can usually be traced to their homes out of doors. The only effectual way of stopping the annoyance or injury from these insects is to destroy the queens living in the nests which they never leave.

OTHER SUBTERRANEAN USES.

The vapor of carbon bisulphid applied at the rates previously recommended is said to have a marked action against certain cryptogamic parasites of plants, though its influence in this direction does not appear to have been much studied. It is also said to be fatal to the nematode worms, which are frequently injurious. In greenhouses these would seem to be particularly susceptible to effective treatment. The vapor of carbon bisulphid is fatal to animal life of all forms if inhaled in sufficient quantity. Within recent years this chemical has come into quite extensive and successful use against a class of small mammals which are common nuisances, if not actual pests, in many parts of the country, and particularly in the West. To Prof. E. W. Hilgard, of the University of California, is given the credit of being the first to employ this remedy against ground squirrels and gophers.* It is a matter of common knowledge that this agent is by far the safest and most efficient known for the destruction of prairie dogs, gophers, pocket gophers, ground squirrels, woodchucks, moles and other pests having similar burrowing habits. The subject is quite an extensive one, and as it is now being given consideration by the Division of Biological Survey, and does not properly come within the province of the Division of Entomology, further comments here are unnecessary.

*Bul. 32, Univ. Cal., "On the Destruction of the Ground Squirrel by the use of Bisulphide of Carbon," 1878.

DESTROYING BORERS IN TRUNKS OF TREES.

Considerable has been written in favor of this use of carbon bisulphid. It is apparent that only the large borers which work in the trunks and lower branches of trees will be good subjects for this treatment. There are usually but few of these in each trunk, and the outlets of such burrows as contain active borers are usually marked by the sawdust and castings which the borers throw out therefrom. Only these burrows should be treated. Clean-cut, empty holes in the trunk indicate that the insect has become adult and left the tree. It is, therefore, a useless waste to inject the liquid into such holes. In peach, plum, apricot and cherry trees (all stone fruits), an abundant exudation of sap through the outlet of the burrow causes a ball of gum, mixed with castings, to collect around the hole. This should be scraped off before the treatment is applied.

Method of treatment.—Having cleaned out the mouth of the hole as well as possible, inject a small quantity of carbon bisulphid and close the hole tightly with a little grafting wax. This will quickly kill the borer and will not injure the tree; it also saves the additional injury which would necessarily be made in cutting out the borer. The saving of time alone will fully pay for the small amount of carbon bisulphide required. The liquid may be conveniently applied by means of a spring-bottomed oil can.

DESTROYING SUCKING INSECTS UPON SMALL PLANTS.

The principal pests included in this group are such insects as plant-lice, which frequently damage melon and squash vines. "The treatment, as successfully practiced by Professors Garman and Smith, consists in covering the young vines with small, tight boxes, 12 to 18 inches in diameter, of either wood or paper, and introducing under each box a saucer containing one or two teaspoonfuls (1 or 2 drams) of the bisulphid. The vines of older plants may be wrapped about the hill and gathered in under larger boxes or tubs, and a greater, but proportional amount of bisulphid used. The covering should be left over the plants for three-quarters of an hour to an hour, and with 50 to 100 boxes a field may be treated with comparative rapidity."

A slight improvement upon the foregoing method of introducing the bisulphid is to bore a hole about 1 inch in diameter in the middle of the top of each box. Under this hole, inside the box, fix a small bunch of cotton waste, rags, or almost any absorbent material capable of taking up somewhat more liquid than it is intended to use; fit a stopper to the hole outside and the box is ready for use. Place it over the plant, being careful to see that the edges set into the dirt all around; remove the stopper; pour in the desired amount of liquid, and place the stopper and leave the vapor to do its work. This obviates the necessity for saucers and saves the trouble of handling more than one thing when moving from vine to vine. The carbon bisulphid might be easily carried in, and poured from, an ordinary gallon oil can such as is used for kerosene.

TREATMENT FOR CLOTHES MOTHS.

The various insects which infest clothing, furs, etc., may be more conveniently and surely destroyed by an application of carbon bisulphid than by anything else. Moth balls, camphor, etc., may do some good by deterring the females from depositing their eggs upon articles treated therewith, but they have no killing power whatever; and if the eggs have already been deposited, the young larvae will feed after hatching as though there were no moth balls or camphor present. Carbon bisulphid, however(will not only keep the adults away, but it will also destroy all stages of the pest infesting the goods. When woolens, furs, and the like are stored away for the summer they may be placed in a tight, paper-lined trunk, a large packing box, or some such receptacle. When all are stored away, place on top a shallow dish holding a few ounces of the liquid, spread some newspapers over the top, and cover tightly. If the box is tight, no further attention will be required; but if not, it will insure safety to repeat the dose every few weeks through the hot weather. It is an excellent plan to provide a large, tight packing chest having a close-fitting cover. Bore a hole through the cover and fasten a small sponge, bunch of cotton waste, or some such thing on the inside. The chest may then be kept tightly closed and carbon bisulphide may be poured through the hole upon the absorbent as may be necessary. Plug the hole with a cork, and all is secure. The cost of such an arrangement will very soon be saved by the convenience and security of the protection thus afforded. Carpets, rugs, robes, etc., can be easily rid of all pests by a few days' inclosure in such a box. The disagreeable odor is much less persistent in the goods than is that of moth balls or tarred paper. If pure carbon bisulphid is used it will not stain or injure the most delicate articles.

USE AGAINST OTHER HOUSEHOLD INSECTS.

Among the many insects which often abound in houses there appear to be very few which are not amenable to successful treatment in the manner already described for buildings. Cockroaches, croton bugs, bed bugs, fleas, carpet beetles, etc., can all be destroyed in tight rooms by a liberal use of the liquid. The holds of ships are frequently cleared of pests in this manner.

DESTROYING MUSEUM PESTS.

Carbon bisulphid is quite generally used for the destruction of a number of insect pests which are included under this heading. Specimens are nearly always inclosed in fairly tight showcases or trays and can be very rapidly treated by inserting the necessary amount of liquid and closing the doors or replacing the covers. In many museums a general annual treatment is given as a measure of safety, even though no enemy is known to be present.

INCIDENTAL EFFECTS OF TREATMENT WITH CARBON BISULPHID.

INFLUENCE UPON THE GROWTH OF CROPS.

As a general rule, the crops grown upon soil treated with carbon bisulphid are very good. This fact suggests several questions: Is the vapor itself a vegetable excitant? Does it produce chemical decompositions which render more assimilable certain nutritive elements already present in the soil? Has it some particular effect upon the humus? Or is its benefit wholly due to the destruction of the lower plant and animal organisms which, living in the soil upon the roots of the plants, steal nourishment therefrom and thus weaken the vitality of their host? None of these questions seems to have been satisfactorily answered. However, it is an acknowledged fact that the growth following treatment is unusually good, and the few records which we find indicate that the increase is considerable. Treatment of a corn field yielded an increase of 46.8 per cent. in the grain and 21.73 per cent. in the stover. Potatoes showed an increase in weight varying from 5.3 per cent. to 38.7 per cent. In a series of experiments upon corn, oats, beets, potatoes and clover much the same results were obtained, but, strange as it may seem, the most marked increase was in the clover. It was found that the vapor was not detrimental to the active bacteria causing the nodules upon the roots of this legume, but rather seemed to favor their multiplication. Furthermore, it was found upon these same plats that the beneficent influence of the treatment was quite apparent the following year, though less marked than it had been the first year.

EFFECT UPON FOOD STUFFS, ETC.

According to the testimony of a large number who have used this insecticide in flouring mills, food stores and like places, the vapor has absolutely no injurious effect upon any food stuff. If the liquid is pure it can even be poured upon such articles, and after thorough exposure to the air not the slightest trace of it will remain. Of course, with impure grades, the liquid should not be poured upon such things, because the excess of sulphur and other impurities therein contained are not volatile, and upon evaporation will be left behind. It is certain that no trace of the vapor which would be absorbed by flour during an exposure thereto could persist through the processes of cooking so as to appear in the food. Owing to the extreme volatility of all the vapors given off even by the impure liquid, they will all be driven out of the flour or dough through the processes of mixing and baking. It can be positively stated that no food stuff has yet been found to be at all injured by an exposure to the vapor of carbon bisulphid.

It is believed that it would be a wise investment to give all mills, warehouses and stores where grains, flour or any food stuffs are kept a thorough annual cleaning, followed by an application of bisulphid some time in early spring. Much if not all this insect injury would thus be avoided and the purity and cleanliness of food materials would be more fully insured.

EFFECT OF THE VAPOR UPON FRUIT.

It has already been stated that the vapor of carbon bisulphid acts as a powerful disinfectant, having the power to preserve meats unchanged for a considerable time. Very recently an Italian, M. F. Sestini, has experimented to determine its effect upon fresh fruits. The substance of his conclusions is as follows:

1. One volume of carbon bisulphid evaporated in 10,000 volumes of air produces no alteration in the character of the fruit during an exposure lasting twenty-four hours. After the treatment flavor is normal and it appears that the perfume of each fruit gains in fineness and intensity.

2. With this dose of carbon bisulphid all the common insects are easily killed in one hour.

3. Under these same conditions the color of the fruits which are not entirely sound becomes deeper, especially upon those parts of their surfaces which have suffered bruises during ripening or from defects in packing; it is thus very easy to choose carefully, rejecting such fruit as could not have been preserved.

PROPERTIES OF CARBON BISULPHID.

Carbon bisulphid is a colorless, watery liquid, formed by the union of two elementary particles of sulphur with one of carbon (charcoal.) Its chemical symbol is CS_2. It is made on a large scale by passing the fumes of burning sulphur over red-hot charcoal. The resulting vapors are condensed to a liquid form by cooling, and the impurities are removed therefrom.

LIQUID PROPERTIES.

The liquid is one-fourth heavier than water, its specific gravity being 1.29 at the freezing temperature of water. It is extremely refractive, so that when its surface is disturbed it reflects the light from the ripples much more strongly than does water. It is very volatile, evaporating with great rapidity when freely exposed to the air. The rapidity of evaporation depends mainly upon the area of the evaporating surface and the temperature of the liquid and the air. It may be retarded by mixing the liquid with various substances, and is wholly prevented by covering the surface of the carbon bisulphid with a layer of water, which, being lighter, floats easily on top just as kerosene does upon water. The rapid evaporation of the liquid takes up a large amount of heat. If a little be poured upon the hand, a burning sensation will be experienced, which, however, is due, not to a burning, but to a cooling process, as may be perceived by touching the spot with the other hand. No harm need be feared from getting it upon the skin. When perfectly pure the liquid has an acrid taste and a rather sweetish, not unpleasant, ethereal odor, quite similar to that of ether or chloroform. Pure carbon bisulphid is completely volatile, and will not injure or stain the finest fabrics. Even when poured directly upon food stuffs their edibility is not at all impaired, and all trace of the odor disappears quickly upon free and full exposure to the air. The ordinary commercial article, however, has a slightly yellowish tinge due to its impurities, which also give it a rank fetid odor that is extremely obnoxious. These impurities add to its poisonous qualities. When the impure article is used, some slight residue may be left after the evaporation of the liquid. For this reason this grade will stain goods, and it should not be poured upon food stuffs, though its vapor will do them no harm. Liquid carbon bisulphid is not at all explosive, so there need be no fear of handling it, provided the cans are perfectly tight. It is best kept in an outhouse where there is no fire and where it is dry, so that the cans will not rust and allow the vapors to escape through leaks. The liquid boils at 115° F., but a few degrees higher than the temperature of the human body. One volume of the liquid is said to give 375 volumes of vapor upon evaporation.

VAPOR PROPERTIES.

The vapor of carbon bisulphid is 2.63 times as heavy as air, and can therefore be poured from one glass to another almost like water. It can be seen flowing down over the edge of an open vessel containing the liquid. Although it diffuses quite rapidly through the air, as can be perceived by its odor, it is evident that the vapor will always tend to work downward more strongly than upward and that it will always be more dense at the lower levels. This point should be borne in mind, as it has an important bearing upon the application of the bisulphid. The vapor, as well as the watery solution, is a powerful disinfectant. Meats will keep in an atmosphere of it for months without change. Lamps have been devised for burning carbon bisulphid in disinfection work, but, as the active disinfectant is the same gas as is formed by burning pure sulphur or brimstone, it can be obtained more cheaply in the latter way.

EFFECTS OF INHALATION OF THE VAPOR.

Concerning the effects of the inhalation of the vapor, we learn from chemical and medical works that the gas is highly poisonous, producing giddiness, vomiting, congestion, coma, and finally death. These of course are its extreme effects. In the ordinary use of carbon bisulphid on a large scale, as in the fumigation of mills, warehouses, etc., where the worker may be more or less exposed to the inhalation of the fumes for some time, only those effects which precede giddiness are likely to be experienced. From his own experience and information obtained from others who have used carbon bisulphid in such work, the writer gleans the following as the effects preceding giddiness: The first appreciable effect is upon the sense of smell. At first the fumes have an extremely disagreeable odor, but this soon seems gradually to disappear, showing that the sense of smell becomes deadened. The other senses seem to become benumbed simultaneously, so that the operator does not realize that anything is the matter with him. The heart beat becomes more and more rapid as the oxygen in the lungs diminishes. The power of thought is very much weakened and the work is continued in a mechanical sort of way. Hearing and sight are also weakened. But before this weakening process has gone far enough to be really dangerous or injurious, the operator will probably feel more or less dizziness. There is no pain or disagreeable sensation; no desire to get out of it, and no sense of suffocation. But when a person has reached this condition it is high time to get out into the fresh air where the ill effects will quickly disappear. Owing to the effect of the gas upon the heart action, it may be well to caution persons having any trouble or weakness about the heart against taking any extended part in the application of the bisulphid. It should be clearly understood by those who use it that the action of the gas is somewhat poisoning as well as suffocating. Should the operator persist in remaining in the room after the dizziness comes on, he will be in danger of falling, and, if not discovered, he will soon suffocate. Even if he should get out safely, the ill effects will be more marked and a severe headache, at least, may ensue. If, upon the approach of dizziness, the operator goes at once to a window, or better still out of doors, an abundance of fresh air will in a few minutes remove all ill effects, and no injury will result from the experience. The inhalation of the fumes can be somewhat retarded by tying a wet handkerchief tightly over the face. This however merely diminishes the amount of air taken into the lungs without affecting the proportion of vapor contained therein. When obliged to enter a room in which the air is charged with any considerable amount of the vapor, the writer makes use of the following simple devise, which is perfectly effectual: A large paper bag (20 quarts or more) is tied tightly around a short piece of tubing of glass, rubber or metal, inserted in its mouth. When inflated the bag contains sufficient air to enable one to respire into it for several minutes without discomfort. Being very light, it can be carried by the tube in the mouth, thus leaving the hands free for any work desired.

This point has been discussed rather fully, not because there is any particular danger or need for fear in handling this insecticide but in order to lessen the fear of its use and to neutralize whatever danger there may be in its application by giving an intelligent understanding of the precise nature and effects of the chemical. When these are known, it can be handled with much greater safety and far less fear than is possible where the user knows there is danger, but does not know just what the danger is. The danger from its use is practically of the same kind as that from gasoline, which is in common use in thousands of homes. Really the danger is very much less, since every precaution is taken to keep carbon bisulphid from the proximity of fire, while gasoline is used principally in connection with fire.

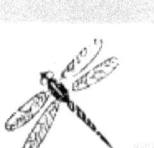

APPENDIX

CHEMICAL EXPERIMENTS WITH CARBON BISULPHID.

The chemical Symbol of carbon bisulphid is CS_2. Its molecules consist of one atom of carbon united with two atoms of sulphur. The specific gravity of the liquid is 1.29. The vapor is 2.63 times as heavy as atmospheric air. The pure article volatizes rapidly and completely when exposed to the air. The liquid boils at 115° F.

The vapor takes fire in air at about 300° F. and burns with a faint blue flame, with difficulty visible in daylight, but evolving considerable heat and decomposing the carbon bisulphid into carbon dioxide (CO_2) and sulphur dioxide (SO_2). The latter is the familiar gas given off by the burning of sulphur matches and is a strongly suffocating poisonous gas, which should not be inhaled. Carbon bisulphid vapor mixed with three times its volume of oxygen, or an amount of air containing that amount of oxygen, forms a mixture which is very highly explosive upon ignition. As 21 per cent. of the air is oxygen, one volume of liquid carbon bisulphid evaporated in 5.357 volumes of air would form such a mixture. An atmosphere composed of one volume of carbon bisulphid vapor to approximately 14.3 volumes of air is liable to violent explosion in the presence of fire of any kind whatever, or a temperature of about 300° F. without flame. We have here about the maximum danger point from explosion in the use of carbon bisulphid.

At the suggestion of the writer, the Division of Entomology requested information from the bureau of Chemistry of the Department of Agriculture on the following points:

(1) Minimum proportional volume of carbon bisulphid vapor inflammable in air.

(2) Minimum proportional volume producing an evident explosion.

(3) Proportion producing most violent explosion and how violent.

(4) Maximum proportional volume giving any explosion.

(5) Temperature of ignition point.

(6) Relative volume of vapor given by evaporation of one volume of liquid carbon bisulphid.

(7) The proportion of vapor of carbon bisulphid in a saturated atmosphere.

(8) The proportion of vapor produced in 1,000 cubic feet of air by the evaporation of 1 pound of carbon bisulphid.

The following is abridged from the report prepared in response to this request in the Bureau of Chemistry by Mr. E. E. Ewell.

AMOUNT OF CARBON BISULPHID IN A SATURATED ATMOSPHERE.

Several factors affect this quantity, but the principle one is temperature. Beginning at the freezing temperature of water, $32°$ F., a series of calculations was made with increments of $9°$ F. in temperature. As will be seen by the accompnaying table, the amount of carbon bisulphid taken up increases most rapidly as the highest temperature is approached.

Amount of carbon bisulphid in a saturated atmosphere at different temperatures.

Temperature.	(avoirdupois) Pounds per 1,000 cubic feet of air.
$32°$ F. ($0°$ C.)	35.8
$41°$ F. ($5°$ C.)	
$50°$ F. ($10°$ C.)	43.9
$59°$ F. ($15°$ C.)	53.5
$68°$ F. ($20°$ C.)	64.6
$77°$ F. ($25°$ C.)	77.6
$86°$ F. ($30°$ C.)	92.4
$95°$ F. ($35°$ C.)	109.3
$104°$ F. ($40°$ C.)	128.6
	150.4

In the following table are given the relative volumes of carbon bisulphid vapor and air in 100 volumes of an atmosphere saturated with vapor at the temperature named and at standard atmospheric pressure:

Relative volumes of CS_2 vapor and air in 100 volumes of a saturated atmosphere (reduced to standard atmospheric pressure) at various temperatures.

Temperature.	Volume of CS_2 vapor	Volume of air
$32°$ F. ($0°$ C.)	16.8	83.2
$41°$ F. ($5°$ C.)	21.1	78.9
$50°$ F. ($10°$ C.)	26.1	73.9
$59°$ F. ($15°$ C.)	32.1	67.9
$68°$ F. ($20°$ C.)	39.2	60.8
$77°$ F. ($25°$ C.)	47.5	52.5
$86°$ F. ($30°$ C.)	57.2	42.8
$95°$ F. ($35°$ C.)	68.4	31.6
$104°$ F. ($40°$ C.)	81.3	18.7

INFLAMMABILITY AND EXPLOSIVENESS OF CARBON BISULPHID VAPOR WITH AIR.

Three series of experiments (two with chemically pure carbon bisulphid, and one with "fuma" carbon bisulphid) were made to determine the inflammability of mixtures of carbon bisulphid (CS_2) vapor with air, and to determine the mixtures which are explosive and the violence of the explosion which takes place when these mixtures are brought in contact with a gas flame.

For the first series an atmosphere saturated with carbon bisulphid (CS) vapor at about 72° F. was prepared. Portions of this saturated atmosphere were transferred to graduated tubes in which it was allowed to mix with varying amounts of air. Ten tubes were prepared in this way, the percentage of the saturated air in the mixture being increased from the first to the tenth. In column 1 of the following table is given the percentage of air saturated with CS_2 vapor at 72° F. used in the mixture in each tube. In column 2 of the table the quantity of carbon bisulphid (grams per liter) in each is stated. In column 3 of the table is given a statement in regard to the degree of inflammability or explosiveness of each of the mixtures.

Inflammability of mixtures of CS_2 with the air.

Per cent. of saturated air in mixture	Grams[a] of liquid CS_2 per liter of the mixture	Inflammability.
5	0.068	Barely inflammable.
10	.135	Inflammable; very slight explosion.
20	.270	Burns with slight explosion.
30	.405	Distinctly stronger explosion.
40	.540	Slight explosion.
50	.675	Mild explosion.
60	.810	Do.
70	.945	Burns almost quietly; slight explosion.
80	1.080	Burns almost quietly, very slight explosion.
100	1.350	Burns quietly.

[a] One pound per 100 cubic feet equals 0.016 grams per liter.

It is to be noted that the explosion which occurred was not violent in any case. The strongest explosions occurred with mixtures containing from 20 to 60 volumes of air saturated with carbon bisulphid vapor at 72° F. mixed with 80 to 40 volumes, respectively, of pure air at the same temperature.

In the second series of experiments a smaller proportion of carbon bisulphid was used in three cases. Five experiments were made. The capacity of five bottles holding 4 liters (about 4 quarts) was obtained with approximate accuracy. For the charging of each bottle the quantity of liquid carbon bisulphid named in the following table was weighed in a small glass-stoppered weighing bottle. A string was tied to the stopper of the weighing bottle, which was then placed in the 4-liter bottle prepared to receive it. When the weighing bottle had reached the bottom of the large bottle, the stopper was removed by a sudden jerk of the string, the string was dropped in the large bottle, and it was quickly closed, the stopper being sealed in immediately with parraffin. This method of preparing the mixtures is more accurate than the one employed for the first series of experiments. The 5 bottles thus charged were allowed to stand for about three hours for the thorough diffusion of the vapor. At about the middle of this period the bottles were inverted in order to facilitate the diffusion. The stopper of each bottle was then carefully removed and a small gas jet burning at the end of a glass tube was inserted in the bottle. The results obtained are indicated in the following table:

Inflammability of mixtures of CS_2 with the air.

No. Bottle	Wt. CS_2 per liter	Wt. CS_2 per 1000 cubic feet	Inflammability
	Grams	Pounds	
1	0.0075	0.47	Not inflammable; slight odor of sulphur dioxid after removal of gas jet.
2	.0182	1.14	No general combustion, a very small blue mantle of burning carbon bisulphid formed around the gas jet.
3	.0461	2.88	No general combustion; blue mantle of burning carbon bisulphid formed around gas jet.
4	.0805	5.02	Inflammable.
5	.1552	9.68	Very inflammable; very slight explosion.

There was no general combustion except in the case of bottles Nos. 4 and 5. In the case of bottles Nos. 3 and 4 the result was very interesting. The mixture of the vapor with air was so dilute that the small gas jet introduced did not heat it hot enough to cause a general combustion, but a zone of combustion extended around the gas jet in every direction in the form of a blue mantle. It is worthy of note that the proportion of carbon bisulphid used in No. 3 (2.88 pounds per 1,000 cubic feet) is more than is ordinarily used in the fumigation of buildings. It must be remembered, however, that when small proportions of carbon bisulphid are used, the quantity in the air near the vessel containing it may be sufficient to cause an explosion if a flame is brought near it, or if the mixture be sufficiently heated by any other means.

The experiments reported above were made with chemically pure carbon bisulphid. The third series of experiments described below was made with the commercial carbon bisulphid known in the market as "fuma," which is largely used as an insecticide. As a comparison of the results will show, the inflammability of this commercial grade of carbon bisulphid is not essentially different from that of the chemically pure substance.

Inflammability of "fuma" carbon bisulphid in mixture with air.

Carbon bi-sulphid sulphid per liter of air	Carbon bi-sulphid sulphid per 1,000 cubic feet of air	Inflammability.
0.002	0.12	Not inflammable.
0.004	0.25	Not inflammable.
0.008	0.50	No general combustion; little or no mantle around gas jet plunged into the mixture.
0.016	1.0	No general combustion; small blue mantle of burning carbon bisulphid formed around gas jet.
0.032	2.0	No general combustion; large blue mantle formed around gas jet and in path of products of combustion.
0.051	3.18	No general combustion; large blue mantle formed around gas jet and in path of products of combustion.
0.084	5.24	Flame traveled slowly to the bottom of the bottle.
0.167	10.42	Very inflammable; scarcely explosive.
0.214	13.35	Very inflammable; Distinct explosion.
0.238	14.85	Strong explosion.
0.356	22.21	Still stronger explosion.
0.463	29.20	Less strong explosion than next preceding mixture.
0.594	37.07	Less strong explosion than next preceding mixture.
0.764	47.67	Less strong explosion than next preceding mixture, but very inflammable.

The temperature at which the vapor ignites when mixed with air is given in chemical text-books as 300° F. Inasmuch as it is sometimes necessary or desirable to use the vapor in rooms in which there are steam pipes or other heating apparatus, it seemed desirable to confirm or redetermine its ignition point. In the experiments made in the Bureau of Chemistry it was found that the vapor could not be ignited at 296.6° F., but twice it took fire at 297.5° F. Of course all higher temperatures would ignite it. Chemically pure carbon bisulphid was used for these experiments.

Mr. C. E. Monroe in an address before the American Chemical Society says: "One of the most striking characteristics of the mixture which this vapor forms with air is its low point of ignition. The tiniest spark, a cinder after it has ceased to glow, or the striking together of two pieces of iron without sparking are sufficient to determine the ignition." In the open air the line of ignition appears to be quite close to that of the liquid itself as is stated by some writers and shown in some experiments by the author; but Dr. C. V. Riley once stated that the vapor ignites "at a great distance from the vessel containing it." In a closed space the ignition depends upon the presence of the vapor in proper proportions and may take place at almost any distance from the liquid. This explosive property of the mixture of the vapor with air is similar to that of alcohol, petroleum products, etc., though its ignition temperature is much lower. The flame extinguishes itself in a closed vessel which does not allow access to the air.

INDEX

Apple Maggot 21
Aphides on Melon Vines 31
Ants 24-83
Alfalfa 24
Bean Weevils 5-6-7
Bisulphide of Carbon as an Insecticide 31-78
Bisulphide of Carbon, Effect on Yield of Crops 49-50-86
Bisulphide of Carbon, Effect on Epidemics 27
Bisulphide of Carbon, Effect on Food Stuffs 87
Bisulphide of Carbon, Effect on Household Insects 54-86
Bisulphide of Carbon, Effect on Preservation of Fruits 87
Bisulphide of Carbon, Properties of 87-95
Bisulphide of Carbon with Vaseline 47
Bisulphide of Carbon Good for Bugs and Rheumatism 73
Bisulphide of Carbon, Brief on General Uses 77
Borers in Trees 33-84
Burrowing Animals 15
Bushes and Trees 20
Cabbage Root Maggot 39-40-41-42-83
Cabbage Plants 45-47
Chicken Lice 7-8-9-10
Clothes Moths 85
Chestnuts, Worms in (Weevil) 21
Cockroaches 54-86
Corn Cribs, Treatment of 22-71
Coccinellidae 31
Crop Yields 49
Corn Ear Riddled by Weevil 73

SATURATED VAPORS OF CARBON BISULPHIDE FROM PROPERTIES OF STEAM AND OTHER VAPORS.

By Cecil H. Peabody.

TABLE III.

Sp. Gr. 1.29. English Units.

Temp. Fahr.	Lbs. press. per sq. in.	Heat of "liquid"	Total heat	Heat of Vaporization	Heat equiv. of int. work	Heat equiv. of ext. work	Specific vol	Density	Temp.
32	2.18	0	162.	162.	149.	13.	28.4	.0353	32
50	3.84	4.15	164.5	160.	146.5	13.47	18.9	.053	50
68	5.76	8.54	167.	158.3	144.4	13.9	12.95	.077	68
86	8.41	12.82	169.3	157.	142.	14.21	9.13	.1095	86
104	11.91	17.16	171.2	154.	139.4	14.6	6.56	.152	104
122	16.58	21.5	173.	152.	137.1	14.9	4.84	.2065	122
140	22.5	26.	175.	149.	134.	15.2	3.64	.275	140
158	30.	30.3	176.7	146.3	131.	15.4	2.67	.361	158
176	39.3	34.8	178.	143.4	128.	15.6	2.15	.466	176
194	50.6	39.4	179.8	140.	124.2	15.8	1.69	.594	194
212	64.4	43.8	181.	137.	121.1	15.9	1.344	.745	212
230	80.5	48.4	182.	133.5	117.5	16.	1.08	.925	230
248	99.5	53.	182.8	130.	113.9	16.1	.882	1.133	248
266	121.8	57.5	183.6	127.	111.	16.1	.725	1.378	266
284	147.	62.2	184.2	122.	106.	16.1	.603	1.665	284
302	176.	66.8	184.6	118.	102	16.0	.505	1.983	302
114	14.7	19.76	172.	153.	138.3	14.7	5.52	.181	114

INDEX CONTINUED

Fr e st	5
Fakes, Bran &	4
Directions ..... for Use In Mills (Cover)	1
The Bar	40
Furniture insects	
For Animals	11
Furs	
Fumigation Houses, Boxes etc.	25-30-31-36-44-45
Fumatorium	9-28-29-30-31
Fumi Carbon Bisulphide	12
Garden Seeds	61
Gophers	11-12-13-15-24
Gr In Bins	22
Greenhouses, Treatment of	29
Grape Root Worm	45
Ground Squirrels	1-18
Ground Hogs	12-16-17-18
Herbariums, Treatment of	26
Hen Fleas	9
Household Insects	34
Insects in Stored Grain	1-50-51-52-73
Instruments for Application	42-43-44-45-81
Insectary	44
Levees, Rats In	20
Melon Insects	83
McGowan Injector	42-43-44-45-83
Mice in Flour House	74
Moles	14-75
Mediterranean Flour Moth	53-56-60-74
Museum Pests	86
Mill Insects	50-53-57-61-86
Pea Weevils	84
Peach Borers	45
Plant Lice	85
Phyloxera	47-78
Pocket Gophers	11
Prairie Dogs	15-19-20-21
Potato Cellars, Rats In	20
Rats	20-64-70
Rice Weevil	55-76
Stored Grain, Insects In	1-2-50-51-52-73
Stave Borers	2
Saddlery, Insects In	27
Skunks	11-15
Squash Bugs	34-35-36-83
Squash Vine Borer	83
Squirrels	15-18
Subterranean Insects	47-48-84
Texas Fleas	10
Trees and Bushes	2
Woodchucks	12-16-17-18-32-75-76
Woolen, Insects In	27
Weevil Fly	62
Weevils	51-52-56
Weasels	15
Weevil in Elevators	50-64
Weevil, Grain Destroyers	68-71
Weevil Kill in the Car	70

Price of "FUMA" F. O. B. Penn Yan, N. Y.

Shipped Only By Freight.

In 100 lb. steel drums, 10 cents per lb. Drums $3.00 extra

In 50 lb. steel drums, 10 cents per lb. Drums $1.50 extra

The drums are returnable, if returned at once and in good condition, at same price, when the freight is prepaid.

Ship the drums to Cascade Mills, N. Y., via the N. Y. C. & H. R. R., and address all correspondence to Penn Yan, N. Y.

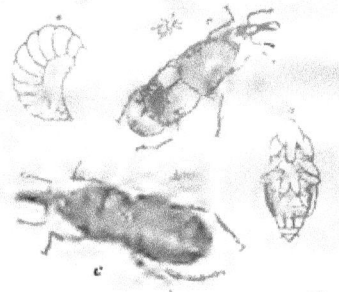

Black Weevil. Grain Weevil, natural size and shown by smaller figures. a, larva, b, pupa.
Cut from Prof. W. G. Johnson in American Elevator and Grain Trade, April 15, 1896.

EDWARD R. TAYLOR
Manufacturing Chemist
PENN YAN, N. Y.

www.ingramcontent.com/pod-product-compliance
Lightning Source LLC
Chambersburg PA
CBHW020859160426
43192CB00007B/994